WEAPON

RUSSIAN MACHINE GUNS SINCE 1945

LEROY THOMPSON
Series Editor Martin Pegler

Illustrated by Adam Hook & Alan Gilliland

OSPREY PUBLISHING
Bloomsbury Publishing Plc
Kemp House, Chawley Park, Cumnor Hill, Oxford OX2 9PH, UK
Bloomsbury Publishing Ireland Limited,
29 Earlsfort Terrace, Dublin 2, Ireland
1385 Broadway, 5th Floor, New York, NY 10018, USA
E-mail: info@ospreypublishing.com
www.ospreypublishing.com

OSPREY is a trademark of Osprey Publishing Ltd

First published in Great Britain in 2025

© Osprey Publishing Ltd, 2025

All rights reserved. No part of this publication may be: i) reproduced or transmitted in any form, electronic or mechanical, including photocopying, recording or by means of any information storage or retrieval system without prior permission in writing from the publishers; or ii) used or reproduced in any way for the training, development or operation of artificial intelligence (AI) technologies, including generative AI technologies. The rights holders expressly reserve this publication from the text and data mining exception as per Article 4(3) of the Digital Single Market Directive (EU) 2019/790

A catalog record for this book is available from the British Library.

ISBN: PB 9781472867599; eBook 9781472867582; ePDF 9781472867612; XML 9781472867605

25 26 27 28 29   10 9 8 7 6 5 4 3 2 1

Index by Rob Munro
Typeset by Lumina Datamatics Ltd.
Printed by Repro India Ltd.

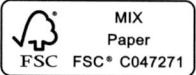

Osprey Publishing supports the Woodland Trust, the UK's leading woodland conservation charity.

To find out more about our authors and books visit www.ospreypublishing.com. Here you will find extracts, author interviews, details of forthcoming events and the option to sign up for our newsletter.

For product safety related questions contact productsafety@bloomsbury.com

Dedication
In memory of my mother, Lorraine Thompson (1912–2001).

Acknowledgments
Thanks to the following for their assistance in preparing this book: Ken Choate, T.J. Mullin, Brian Peek, and John Ross (RIP).

Artist's note
Readers may care to note that the original paintings from which the battlescene artworks in this book were prepared are available for private sale. All reproduction copyright whatsoever is retained by the publishers. All inquiries should be addressed to:

scorpiopaintings@btinternet.com

The publishers regret that they can enter into no correspondence upon this matter.

Front-cover photographs. Above: A PKM. (© Royal Armouries). Below: Pictured in 2016, a Ukrainian soldier demonstrates firing the RPK from the prone position. (US Army/Public Domain)

Title-page photograph: A Syrian insurgent fires a DShKM during an exercise at Babisqa, October 2020. While this prominent position would allow interdiction of enemy movement along a highway, the gunner would be easily eliminated by a helicopter gunship. (dpa picture alliance/Alamy Stock Photo)

CONTENTS

INTRODUCTION 4

DEVELOPMENT 6
Small arms adaptation and innovation

USE 32
A universal battlefield presence

IMPACT 67
Global influence

CONCLUSION 75

BIBLIOGRAPHY 78

INDEX 80

INTRODUCTION

An Iraqi soldier wields an RPK during joint operations with the US Army's 2d Cavalry Regiment in Baghdad, October 2007. A second magazine is fastened to the one in use to enable a quick change in combat. He appears to have found a position offering some cover and to have placed the bipod on a surface offering support. Grasping the foregrip will aid in controlling the weapon. Overall, he displays good tactical awareness. (Tech Sergeant Andrew M. Rodier, USAF/Wikimedia/Public Domain)

Russian small arms after the two 1917 revolutions were designed to be durable, simple so they could be readily fired and maintained by conscript troops, and easy and inexpensive to produce. Ease of production did not necessarily mean that reliability was sacrificed, however. For example, many weapons would be produced with a chromed bore to limit the effects of firing corrosive ammunition. Production also sometimes allowed for repurposing of parts from another weapon. For example, rejected barrels for the 7.62×54mmR Mosin-Nagant M1891 bolt-action rifle could still be used in 7.62×25mm submachine guns (SMGs).

In June 1941, the Soviet armed forces retained the venerable PM M1910/30 medium machine gun (MMG) alongside the recently adopted DS-39 MMG, but the latter weapon was found wanting and replaced in 1943 by the SG-43 MMG. All three of these weapons used the standard 7.62×54mmR rifle cartridge, as did the standard squad support weapon, the DP light machine gun (LMG). The DShK-38 heavy machine gun (HMG), however, represented a new element of Soviet firepower, chambering the 12.7×108mm round and drawing inspiration from the US .50-caliber Browning M2 HMG.

Although some of these designs would remain in use with Soviet troops well into the postwar era, the Cold War would see the development of new machine guns to confront new enemies. While Soviet military doctrine continued to be shaped by the prospect of all-out warfare in Europe against the Western Allies and then NATO, the Soviet–Afghan War (1979–89) had a major influence on machine-gun development and tactics as the Soviet Army found itself fighting a counterinsurgency war in rugged terrain, rather than the anticipated conflict against NATO in which tanks and artillery would be preeminent. Whether mounted on armored vehicles or helicopters or used by dismounted troops, machine guns would prove invaluable in ambushes and in defending against Mujahideen ambushes. Following the demise of the Soviet Union in 1991,

A Chechen fighter with a PK variant in Grozny, January 1995. Note the rough finish to the pistol grip and the cover on the buttstock. (David Brauchli/Alamy Stock Photo)

the Chechen Wars (1994–96 and 1999–2009) once again made operations by smaller infantry units and the tactical flexibility of machine guns especially relevant.

It is important not just to enumerate the various post-World War II machine guns but to also to examine how their development and use fit into Soviet tactical doctrine during the Cold War and possible combat across the North German Plain but also in Afghanistan, Chechnya, and Ukraine as well as in insurgencies fomented by Russian clients. Influences of other weapons designs, such as the German MG 42 general-purpose machine gun (GPMG), must be examined, as must how "soldier proof" and "user friendly" the weapons actually proved to be in the hands of Russian troops, many of them conscripts. As a corollary, the author – who has had experience firing most modern Russian machine guns – discusses the strengths and weaknesses of the designs from the point of view of the individual combatant who must carry the weapon, emplace it, load the feed device, and engage the enemy.

DEVELOPMENT
Small arms adaptation and innovation

An Egyptian Marine with an RPD during Exercise *Bright Star*, August 1985. The 100-round drum offers a way of carrying substantial ammunition ready for use in sandy or dusty environments. (Captain Mark Beberwyck/Wikimedia/Public Domain)

THE LEGACY OF WORLD WAR II

The Wehrmacht launched Operation *Barbarossa*, Germany's invasion of the Soviet Union, on June 22, 1941. Despite having fought the Winter War (1939–40) against Finland – a conflict that was heavily dependent on infantry – the Soviet Union had lagged far behind Germany in the development of infantry-support automatic weapons. The primary Soviet machine guns were the belt-fed PM M1910 MMG and the Degtyaryov DP-27 LMG.

Adopted in 1910, the PM M1910 (PM: *Pulemyot Maksima*; "Maxim's machine gun") continued in use with the Imperial Russian Army through World War I, then was used by both sides during the Russian Civil War (1917–22). At the end of that conflict, the Red Army retained the PM M1910, but needed a more portable weapon and in large quantities. Because the Soviet Union had a large amount of 6.5×50mm ammunition acquired from Japan during World War I, along with Arisaka rifles, early designs of a lighter machine gun were chambered for this round. Noted weapons designers V.G. Fedorov and V.A. Degtyaryov designed LMGs and MMGs that used a short-recoil, locked-breech design chambering the 6.5×50mm cartridge. These weapons were not adopted, however.

The PM M1910 was reliable, though its water jacket and wheeled mount increased the weight substantially to 62.6kg. The weight certainly made the PM M1910 stable and its 7.62×54mmR chambering gave it range and killing power; and because it took what was the standard Soviet rifle cartridge, the supply of ammunition was straightforward. The PM M1910 did not, however, lend itself well to providing supporting fire during an assault or a retreat in which troops would be moving quickly. A modernized version, the PM M1910/30, entered service in 1930.

Pictured in 2022, Ukrainian territorial troops train with (left) the Maxim PM M1910 MMG and (right) the DPM LMG. (www.mil.gov.ua/Wikimedia/CC BY 4.0 & armyinform.com.ua/Wikimedia/CC BY 4.0)

An interesting Russian variant of Maxim's MMG was often referred to as the "tractor-cap" or "snow-cap" Maxim, which had a larger hole atop the water jacket to enable snow to be used for cooling the weapon. Maxim MMGs continued in use with Soviet troops through World War II and have been seen in use by both Russian and Ukrainian troops during the current war between those two countries.

For close infantry support, Soviet weapon designers developed the DP (*Pulemyot Degtyaryova Pekhotny*; "Degtyaryov's infantry machine gun"), a gas-operated, open-bolt LMG which fed from a top-mounted 47-round pan magazine. A Degtyaryov design chambered for the ubiquitous 7.62×54mmR cartridge, the weapon was known variously as the DP, DP-27, or DP-28. Other features included a pistol grip, integral bipod, and conical flash hider. Weight was 11.5kg with a loaded magazine, which made the weapon portable enough to be carried into a combat by a gunner. Although the pan magazines were slow to load, if enough of them were available, the DP-27 could provide sustained fire. For the early 1930s, it was a relatively effective LMG. Tank and aircraft variants of the DP-27, designated the DT (*Degtyaryova Tankovy*; "tank-mounted Degtyaryov") and DA (*Degtyaryova Aviatsionny*; "aircraft-mounted Degtyaryov") respectively, were developed, though the drum magazine (even the 60-round version developed for the DA) limited the DA's effectiveness in aerial combat.

Always important in Soviet-era machine-gun designs, the DP had relatively few parts and was sturdy and simple to operate. Though the DP-27 would remain in production from 1928 to the 1950s, it did have some design deficiencies, which were corrected or mediated over the weapon's lifespan: the pan magazines were prone to damage and time-consuming to load; the bipod proved too fragile in continuous combat use, when an infantryman might slam it into the ground while going prone; and location of the recoil spring close to the barrel resulted in the loss of spring temper as a result of the barrel overheating. A version designated the DPM (M: *Modernizirovanny*; "modernized") entered service in 1943–44; it had a more robust bipod and the recoil spring was now located in a tube at the rear of the receiver, necessitating the addition of a pistol grip. Despite its flaws, the DP and its variants may still be found in use with insurgents in some parts of the world.

Prior to the German invasion, the Soviet Union had developed a new MMG, the Degtyaryov DS-39 (*Degtyaryova Stankovyy Obraztsa 1939 Goda*; "Degtyaryov with mount of 1939"), once again chambered for the 7.62×54mmR cartridge. This air-cooled design was lighter than the PM M1910/30, weighing only 14.5kg without its tripod. Fed from a 250-round canvas ammunition belt, the DS-39 offered a cyclic rate of 1,200rd/min, seemingly a distinct upgrade from the PM M1910/30, as was its relatively light-weight tripod (though it later proved fragile in combat), resulting in adoption of the DS-39 as a replacement for the PM M1910/30 in 1939. The combination of the canvas belt and the 12.7×108mm rimmed cartridge adversely affected reliability, however. Tearing of cartridge cases and bullet separation from the cartridge case when bullets were pulled from the belt was reportedly the major issue. The DS-39 proved less reliable in combat during the harsh conditions encountered in the Soviet Union, and after the German invasion, production was halted and factories once again began producing the PM M1910/30.

The SG-43 (*Stankovyy Pulemyot Sistemy Goryunova*; "Mounted machinegun, Goryunov design"), a design from P.M. Goryunov, proved an effective MMG. Gas-operated and air-cooled, it used a tilting breechblock locking system, had a three-position gas regulator, and offered a quick-change barrel, all of which, when combined with a 250-round canvas ammunition belt, allowed effective sustained fire. The feed mechanism was complicated in that a cartridge had to be withdrawn from the belt to the rear then pushed into the breech. This feed system was necessitated by use of the 7.62×54mmR rimmed cartridge. Although this feed mechanism sounds complicated, the SG-43 actually proved to be reliable. It was designed to use standard PM ammunition belts and could also use any standard PM mount.

Unlike many machine guns, the SG-43 was designed for right-hand feed. An excellent ergonomic feature was that the cocking handle was of the spade type and located in the horizontal position beneath the standard spade grip. The barrel was heavy and had a chromed bore. The weapon could hold up to sustained firing well, but it also allowed for the quick change of barrels. An extremely important advantage of the SG-43 was that it was far faster and cheaper to produce than previous machine guns – a real boon in equipping forces such as the burgeoning Red Army. The SG-43 still used a wheeled mount, however, which gave the weapon a weight of 54.9kg when mounted.

After the end of World War II, the SG-43 was improved and re-designated the SGM. An improved dust cover and barrel lock were incorporated and a finned barrel was adopted for better cooling during sustained fire. The SGM remained in service with the Soviet armed forces into the 1960s. The SGMT was a version designed for mounting on tanks and other armored fighting vehicles and, hence, had a solenoid firing system.

One other weapon should be mentioned when discussing Soviet machine guns in service with the Red Army during World War II. The 12.7×108mm DShK was (and is) a true HMG suitable for use in the antiaircraft role and also as a vehicle-mounted HMG. On a heavy wheeled mount it was also used as an infantry-support weapon.

Egyptian Marines armed with an SG-43 participate in Exercise *Bright Star*, August 1985. Note the fluted barrel, likely indicating that the weapon was manufactured under license in Egypt. (Sergeant Major C.B. Simmons/Wikimedia/Public Domain)

GERMAN INFLUENCE

The weapons just discussed and their effectiveness in combat during World War II would affect postwar Soviet machine-gun development, but so would innovative German weapons such as the MG 34, MG 42, and StG 44.

Germany entered World War II with one of the world's best MMGs – arguably the best – in the 7.92×57mm MG 34, generally accepted as the first modern GPMG. Designed by Mauser, it was a mix of proven features used on other machine guns and innovations in design. Among the features taken from the 7.92×57mm MG 13 LMG, which had entered service in 1930, was the use of finger position on the trigger as a selector, a pull high on the trigger allowing semiautomatic fire and low on the trigger allowing full-automatic fire. (Among current weapons that use this system is the Austrian Steyr AUG bullpup assault rifle.) The MG 34's locking system was similar to that of the 7.92×57mm MG 30 Solothurn LMG in that the MG 30 employed a rotating ring to lock the barrel and bolt together, while the MG 34 utilized a bolt head, which rotated and locked into the barrel extension.

New features of the MG 34 included a quick and sure method of barrel change, ease of field stripping for maintenance or repair, use of bayonet catches to secure components, a durable polymer stock, and a combination recoil booster, barrel bearing, and flash hider. During World War II, various upgrades were incorporated in the MG 34 based on combat experience, including a heavier barrel jacket for mounting on armored vehicles, versions with shorter barrels, and using a spur trigger only capable of full-auto fire.

The MG 34's metallic-link ammunition "belt" proved easy to load by hand if necessary, though a loader was available; and very reliable 50-round drums and 75-round saddle drums were available, though the saddle drums could not incorporate a belt. Tabs at the end of each belt allowed sections to be joined together for more continuous fire.

As a boon to the Wehrmacht's logistic system, the MG 34 was chambered for the standard 7.92×57mm cartridge. Cyclic rate was 800–900rd/min, though gunners were trained to fire short bursts to keep the weapon from overheating. As World War II machine guns went, the MG 34 was quite portable, weighing 12kg with its bipod mounted; but when firing from an emplaced position, the Lafette 34 tripod added 20kg. The weapon was 1,219mm long with a barrel length of 627mm. With the bipod, the MG 34 proved a portable squad automatic weapon that could lay down a lot of fire. It also made an excellent weapon for mounting on vehicles or motorcycles. In fact, after the adoption of the MG 42, the MG 34 remained in production for mounting on tanks and other vehicles as their mounts had been designed to take the MG 34.

The MG 34 was a revolutionary machine-gun design, but after using it in combat, the Germans developed an improved design that resulted in the 7.92×57mm MG 42 GPMG. With a high cyclic rate of 1,200rd/min, the MG 42 would have overheated quickly when used to provide sustained fire; hence, a new quick-change barrel system based on previous designs from Breda of Italy and Stecke of Poland was incorporated. Although the MG 34 had offered an example of German quality and machining to be admired, the need for a massive number of machine guns for use on the Eastern Front inspired the use of stampings and pressings in the MG 42. This allowed not only faster and less expensive production, but fabrication at multiple factories. Among other features of the MG 42 were a shorter (565mm) barrel and full-automatic fire only. It used the same bipod as the MG 34 and the innovative Lafette 42 tripod still in use on MG 42-derived machine guns today. The MG 42 weighed about 0.45kg less than the MG 34.

Another innovative German design, which would have some influence on postwar Soviet weapons, was the StG 44 assault rifle. Developed by Hugo Schmeisser, this was the world's first truly successful assault rifle. Its 7.92×33mm *Kurz* ("short") cartridge was an intermediate round, less powerful than the full-powered rifle rounds in general use during World War II. Because the 7.92×33mm *Kurz* cartridge was more compact and lighter than a typical battle-rifle cartridge, more rounds could be carried by the infantryman. The StG 44's operating system employed a gas-operated, long-stroke piston, with a closed tilting bolt. Both the AK-47 assault rifle and the Soviet 7.62×39mm cartridge were influenced by the StG 44, as were postwar Soviet machine guns such as the PK GPMG and RPK LMG.

BELOW LEFT
An Iranian soldier armed with the MG3, a West German derivative of the MG 42 GPMG widely supplied to Iran and other countries across the world, *c*.1981. (Hamsharionline.ir/Wikimedia/Public Domain)

BELOW RIGHT
East German police armed with the StG 44 assault rifle, October 1955. Weighing only 4.59kg unloaded and measuring 940mm in overall length, the StG 44 was easily carried, yet it gave the user impressive firepower: 500–600rd/min on full-auto. Its effective range on full-auto was rated at about 300m, however; and its 30-round detachable box magazine also limited how long fire could be sustained. (Bundesarchiv, Bild 183-33349-0002/Giso Löwe/CC BY-SA 3.0 de)

A NEW CARTRIDGE

Soviet experimentation with an intermediate cartridge began in mid-1943 with the goal of adopting a semiautomatic carbine, a select-fire rifle, and an LMG chambered for the new round. The new cartridge was first adopted in December 1943, but its initial 41mm case length meant that it did not have quite the same specifications as the ubiquitous 7.62×39mm cartridge so widely used today. Limited production began of the 7.62×41mm cartridge in 1944, with testing continuing until 1947, when changes were made to improve its accuracy and penetration. The resulting cartridge was similar to the 7.62×39mm cartridge used today.

The year 1947 also appeared in the designation of the AK-47, which was chambered for the 7.62×39mm cartridge. Companion weapons, which would also chamber that cartridge, were the SKS battle rifle and the RPD LMG; but though all three weapons were chambered for the same cartridge, each weapon owed its development to a different inventor. The SKS (*Samozaryadny Karabin Sistemy Simonova*; "Simonov's self-loading carbine system") was designed by S.G. Simonov, who had been developing semiautomatic rifles since the 1920s. The AK-47 was developed by M.T. Kalashnikov and would go on to become the world's most widely used infantry rifle. Development of the RPD (*Ruchnoy Pulemyot Degtyaryova*; "Degtyaryov hand-held machine gun") began in 1943, though it was not adopted until 1948 and substantial numbers did not reach Soviet troops until 1953. With the adoption of the AK-47 in 1949, the RPD would share the standard small-arms cartridge with the assault rifle, thus easing logistics for combat units.

The 7.92×33mm *Kurz* cartridge (left) for the German StG 44, which influenced development of the 7.62×39mm cartridge (right) for the AK-47. (Author)

THE DShK

An important Soviet machine-gun design from before World War II that would carry over into the postwar Soviet armed forces was the 12.7×108mm DShK HMG. The Red Army first became interested in an HMG during the 1920s. In 1927, development began of a large-caliber machine gun for use as an antiaircraft weapon but also with armor-piercing (AP) ammunition for use against light armored vehicles. Chosen for use in this new machine gun was the 12.7×108mm rimless cartridge. Various specialized loads would be developed in this caliber, including AP and armor-piercing incendiary (API). This was not the original choice of chambering, however, as a round based on the .50-caliber Vickers cartridge was evaluated but rejected.

By 1933, a machine gun intended to fire the new cartridge had been designed by Degtyaryov. This early HMG, designated the DK (*Degtyaryrov Krupnokaliberny*, "Degtyaryov large caliber"), was essentially an upscaled version of the DP-27 LMG (Popenker & Williams 2008: 327). The DK was gas-operated and air-cooled. It was an open-bolt design, which aided in cooling. Ammunition was fed from a 30-round top-loading drum similar to that employed on the DP-27.

The 30-round drum proved to be too heavy and too low in rounds fired per minute for active antiaircraft use, however, and was replaced by a belt-feed system in 1938 on the DShK-38 model of the weapon. The barrel was not readily changeable, requiring a wrench to unscrew it after first unscrewing a locking stud. The belt-feed system employed a rotary-feed block with depressions for the cartridges. This feed system, which employed a lever system similar to that of the RP-46, was developed by G.S. Shpagin (the "Sh" in the weapon's designation), best known for his work on the iconic PPSh-41 SMG. Two rear sights were included, one for antiaircraft use and the other for ground use.

Spade-type handles allowed good control of the DShK-38's heavy recoil. Another ergonomically useful feature was the incorporation of a charging handle, located below the spade grip but perpendicular to it. In case of damage or another problem affecting use of the charging handle, a disc with a hole in it was located on the right side of the receiver so that an empty 12.7×108mm cartridge case could be inserted to act as an improvised cocking handle. A safety lever was also located on the right side of the receiver.

Initially, the DShK-38 had a rather complicated muzzle brake, which also appears to have been somewhat fragile. In 1944, this was replaced with a simpler and stronger muzzle brake. An improved version of the DShK-38 employing the new muzzle brake and an improved feed system was designated the DShK-38-46 or (sometimes) the DShKM in 1946.

The DShKM and earlier versions were not conducive to quick movement. The weapon itself weighed 34kg and was 1,625mm in overall length; when affixed to the wheeled mount, the weight rose to 157kg. Movement of the mounted weapon took the effort of at least two men. On the positive side, the wheeled mount was designed for versatility as it could be converted into a tripod for antiaircraft use. On the DShK-38, the wheeled mount was also not considered sufficiently stable. It should be noted, though, that the DShKM was not noted for its accuracy. Nevertheless, much as with US antimateriel rifles such as the Barrett, the 12.7×108mm cartridge was employed in the subsequent KSVK antimateriel sniping rifle.

Although it is no longer being manufactured, the DShKM remains in service today and, along with the M2, is among the world's preeminent HMGs. It saw extensive use by PAVN and VC forces during the Vietnam War, and accounted for a high percentage of US helicopter losses during that conflict. The DShKM continues in use at the time of writing, in Ukraine against Russian forces and in other insurgencies around the world.

A DShKM fitted to a T-54 main battle tank in Czechoslovakia, August 1968. The DShKM ranks alongside the US .50-caliber M2 as the longest-serving and most effective HMG in the world. Estimates are that up 1,000,000 examples have been produced. The DShKM would eventually be adopted by nearly 100 countries, primarily in the Soviet sphere of influence and Developing World. Images of DShKMs truck-mounted on "Technicals" have become ubiquitous from Afghanistan, Iraq, and other conflicts in Africa and the Middle East. It also has the distinction of having earned an affectionate name from its Russian users – *Dushka* ("beloved one"). (CTK/Alamy Stock Photo)

THE RP-46

In an attempt to field a more effective LMG – or maybe a stopgap MMG – in the immediate postwar years, the RP-46 (*Rotnyi Pulemyot 1946*; "Company machine gun model 1946"), an improved version of the DP-27, was developed. Upgrades to the DP-27 had begun during World War II when a sturdier bipod affixed to the cooling jacket was added along with a recoil-spring tube, which projected from the rear of the receiver. This tube required the addition of a pistol grip that helped control the weapon in full-auto fire. The result was the DPM.

In 1946 the most significant upgrade to the DP-27 took place when a belt-feed system similar to that of the DShKM was added. The feed tray of this system was attached above the former feed system for the pan magazine. If so desired, the belt-feed system could be removed and the DP-27 would still function with pans. As with other Soviet belt-feed systems in weapons chambered for the 7.62×54mmR rimmed cartridge, the RP-46's system had to pull the cartridge from the ammunition belt (the same non-disintegrating belt used with the PM M1910/30) with a "claw" and lower it onto the feed tray for chambering.

The RP-46 also incorporated a changeable barrel with a handle, thus allowing removal and replacement with another barrel for sustained fire. A figure of 500 rounds of continuous fire was generally accepted before the RP-46's barrel overheated. Another aid to sustained fire was a three-position adjustable gas system.

This photo of a New York State National Guardsman firing a DShK variant during exchange training with Ukrainian forces offers a good view of the weapon's muzzle brake diverting flame to the sides. (DVIDS/Public Domain)

An RP-46 on display in the United States, July 1988. An important advantage of the RP-46 over the DP-27 was portability. Although at 10kg the RP-46 was 2.5kg heavier than the DP-27, the overall load for the gunner was less, as the RP-46 with a 250-round box magazine was actually 10kg lighter than a DP-27 with five or six 47-round pans. Of course, the greatest advantages of the RP-46 were the range and striking power granted by the weapon's 7.62×54mmR chambering (Corporal D.A. Haynes/Wikimedia/Public Domain)

THE RPD

The 7.62×39mm RPD was chosen as the new Soviet LMG over designs by Simonov and A.I. Sudayev. Degtyaryov had previously designed the long-serving DP-27, for which the RPD would be a replacement. The RPD would also be the last of Degtyaryov's 82 weapons designs to be adopted.

One of the most distinctive Degtyaryov design features carried over to the RPD is the use of flaps on the sides of the bolt that cam into locking points on the receiver. The bolt carrier incorporates angled surfaces that control the locking or unlocking of these flaps. A fully automatic weapon, the RPD employs a gas-operated, long-stroke piston action. It fires from an open bolt, an important feature to aid cooling since the barrel is not of a quick-change design. Ejection of fired cartridge cases is downward through an opening in the bolt carrier and receiver. The RPD's "club foot" buttstock houses the recoil spring.

There were five versions of the RPD, though the changes were not dramatic. The first version had a "female" gas piston with a "male" gas spigot and lacked a dust cover, but incorporated a reciprocating cocking handle, and a windage knob to the right of the rear sight. The second version switched to a male gas piston with a female gas cylinder and placed the windage knob to the left of the rear sight. The third version added a dust cover over the feed port and a non-reciprocating cocking handle. The fourth version, known as the RPDM, had an extended gas cylinder, a friction roller on the side of the piston, and a buffer within the buttstock. The fifth version added a folding cover for the feed system and a cleaning rod contained in the buttstock.

As was typical with many Soviet weapons, the RPD has a chrome-lined barrel to help mitigate the use of corrosive ammunition. The RPD's

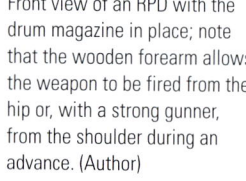

Front view of an RPD with the drum magazine in place; note that the wooden forearm allows the weapon to be fired from the hip or, with a strong gunner, from the shoulder during an advance. (Author)

ABOVE LEFT
Close-up of the RPD's feed ramp. (Author)

ABOVE RIGHT
A left-side view of the RPD's feed port and rear sight. (Author)

safety consists of a lever, located on the right side of the receiver for manipulation of the trigger finger, which blocks the bolt when rotated to the safe position. A three-position valve can be operated with a tool included in the machine-gun tool kit. The valve allows the gas flow to be adjusted when the RPD becomes fouled. It is relatively easy to strip the RPD into major parts, but the receiver and barrel remain together.

Along with cartridge compatibility, portability was a great advantage of the RPD. Although still substantially heavier (9kg) than the AK-47 (4.79kg), an RPD with a 100-round ammunition belt inserted in a drum could still be carried by a fit machine-gunner. Arguably, the most important aspect of the RPD was its use of the intermediate 7.62×39mm cartridge.

The RPD only remained in front-line service with the Soviet armed forces until 1961, though versions produced by China, as well as the Soviet Union, saw extensive use in various proxy wars. During the Vietnam War (1955–75), US troops faced the RPD in the hands of the People's Army of Vietnam (PAVN) and Viet Cong (VC). To replace the RPD and have an LMG that would fire the same round as the SKS and AK-47, the RPK was adopted.

THE KPV

During World War II, some elements of the Red Army requested an even more powerful HMG that would chamber the 14.5×114mm round used in the PTRD and PTRS antitank rifles. Initially designed in 1944 by S.V. Vladimirov, the resulting weapon was designated the KPV (*Krupnokaliberniy Pulemyot Vladimirova*; "Vladimirov's large-caliber machine gun"). Introduced in 1949, it was initially intended primarily for antiaircraft use, but also served as a mounted HMG for armored fighting vehicles, in which case it was designated the KPVT. Its relatively short overall length of 600mm enhanced its appeal for vehicle usage. The KPVT has a heavier barrel jacket and can be fitted with a solenoid firing system. An antiaircraft version was designated the ZPU (*Zenitnaya Pulemotnaya Ustanovka*; "antiaircraft machine-gun mount") and could be encountered in one-, two-, and four-barrel versions. For use on patrol boats and other light craft, it was designated the 14.5mm MTPU (*Morskaya Tumbovaya Pulemotnaya Ustanovka*; "naval machine-gun mount").

The KPV employed an air-cooled, gas-assisted, short-recoil operating system with a muzzle booster that enhanced the gas pressure; and it had a locked breech and a rotating locking bolt. Cyclic rate was 600rd/min, high enough to allow effective use in the antiaircraft role. Bursts of fire

Two KPVTs mounted on an SU-122-54 assault gun, displayed at Kubinka, Russia, 2015. This pairing of KPVTs offers the versatility of engaging while "buttoned up" or being able to fire in a wider arc when using the top-mounted weapon. (Uwe Brodrecht/Wikimedia/ CC BY-SA 2.0)

Pictured in Syria in May 2016, this Toyota pickup has a KPVT mounted behind the cab. In insurgencies around the world, the DShKM and KPVT are frequently mounted in this way. (L-BBE/Wikimedia/CC BY 3.0)

would have normally been relatively short, however, given the heavy recoil and the use of a metallic linked ammunition belt holding 40 rounds that could feed from either the right or left. As with Soviet machine guns chambered for the 7.62×54mmR round, a two-stage feed system was employed in which cartridges had to be pulled from the belt by a "claw," then inserted into a slot on the breech face. Durability was enhanced by use of a chrome-plated bore. The barrel could also be removed relatively quickly.

The KPV is an extremely powerful weapon. For example, the US .50-caliber Browning round typically develops between 17.6kJ and 19kJ of muzzle energy depending on the bullet weight, while the KPV's 14.5×114mm round develops between 30kJ and 31.2kJ of muzzle energy, again depending on the bullet weight. Maximum effective range for the KPV is usually given as 3,000–4,000m, though unimpeded the bullet would travel up to twice that distance and still retain lethality. An array of ammunition types was available for the KPV including high-explosive incendiary – tracer (HEI-T) and API.

The weight of the KPV unmounted was 49.1kg. Standard infantry mounts available were wheeled and of the type used for artillery pieces, and could be towed into fixed positions. Although originally intended for deployment as an infantry weapon, the KPV was found to be too heavy and cumbersome for that role. In later usage, it would be set up on remote weapons stations. Because of the difficulties in moving the KPV during infantry advances, by the 1960s it had been relegated primarily to antiaircraft and antiarmor use mounted on BTR armored personnel carriers and BRDM armored amphibious vehicles.

THE RPK

As a replacement for the DPM and RPD, the Soviet armed forces adopted a new LMG in 1961. Designated the RPK (*Ruchnoy Pulemyot Kalashnikova*; "Kalashnikov's hand-held machine gun"), this weapon was chambered for the same 7.62×39mm cartridge as the AK-47. The RPK used the Kalashnikov-action gas-operated, long-stroke piston with rotating bolt located above the barrel. The operating system of the RPK was the same as that of the AK-47/AKM assault rifle, though there were some changes to allow the RPK to function at longer ranges and with more sustained fire. These changes included a beefier receiver, a heavier and longer chrome-lined barrel, sights more suitable for longer ranges, and a bipod. The buttstock is similar to that of the RPD and is better suited to sustained firing from the prone position. Although the RPK will take standard 30-round AK-47 magazines, 40-round box magazines and 75-round drum magazines are available to allow more sustained fire. Particularly for the Soviet Army with many conscripts, the use of both the AKM and RPK allowed for ease of training as both weapons field-strip basically the same, and also meant a squad member could replace the gunner if the latter was killed or wounded.

The RPKS (S: *Skladnoy*; "folding") has a folding stock and is more suited for airborne or *spetsnaz* usage. Along with the adoption of the AK-74, a 5.45×39mm version of the RPK designated the RPK-74 was also adopted for which a 45-round magazine was developed. As with the RPKS, there is an airborne/*spetsnaz* RPKS-74. The RPK-74M modernized version has polymer furniture and a siderail for mounting optics among other upgrades. Other versions designed to mount a night-vision device (NVD) on a siderail were developed and designated, depending on the type of NVD, the RPKN or RPKSN.

Actually, the RPK was developed along with the AKM, the product-improved version of the AK-47. The RPK/RPK-74 was designed as a "base of fire" weapon for the Soviet infantry squad, while the PKM GPMG was intended for use at infantry platoon or company level. Though the functioning of the RPK is the same as the AKM and their

BELOW LEFT
A view of the RPK's rear sight with graduations to 1,000m. (Author)

BELOW RIGHT
A close-up of the RPK's selector switch; note that it is designed to operate in the same manner as the AK-47 to help make it more "soldier proof." The positions are (from top): safe; middle, full-automatic; and semiautomatic. (Author)

An RPK-74 on its bipod along with 30- and 45-round magazines. (Author)

magazines will interchange, there are some differences designed to allow the RPK to function more reliably in the LMG role. For example, its receiver is fabricated of 1.5mm-thick steel as opposed to 1mm for the AKM; the receiver is 20mm longer; the chrome-lined barrel measures 590mm compared to the AKM's 415mm barrel and is heavier; and both the "club foot" buttstock (derived from the RPD) and bipod give a better gripping surface for the support hand when firing from the prone position. Better rear sights with settings to 1,000m aid longer-range accuracy.

The standard magazine for the RPK was the 40-round AK-47 type, which could also be used in the AKM. Standard AKM 30-round magazines could also be used reliably. Some gunners carried a 30-round magazine in the RPK when moving as it was less likely to snag while moving through cover and could be brought into action more quickly. Also available was a 75-round drum, but it was slow to load and rattled; hence it was not very popular. Another advantage of the 40-round magazine over the drum was that the time spent changing magazines limited the duration of bursts of fire, which gave a little time for the barrel to cool. Gunners were trained to only fire two 40-round magazines per minute to prevent overheating. As the RPK fires from a closed bolt, "cook-offs" (thermal-induced firing of cartridges rather than from a trigger pull) were more likely if lengthy bursts were fired.

An RPK-74N2 fitted with a 1PN589 night scope. Weighing 2.1kg, the 3.5× IPN589 is a "passive" night optic, i.e. not having an active illuminator in the infrared band. (Vitaly V. Kuzmin/Wikimedia/CC BY-SA 4.0)

THE RPK REVEALED

7.62mm RPK light machine gun

1. Buttplate
2. Accessory case
3. Case spring
4. Receiver cover
5. Rear sight
6. Handguard
7. Gas tube
8. Gas piston
9. Barrel
10. Front sight
11. Barrel bushing
12. Bipod
13. Forearm
14. Drum magazine
15. Trigger guard
16. Pistol grip
17. Buttstock
18. Return spring
19. Bolt and bolt carrier
20. Firing pin
21. Magazine release
22. Hammer spring

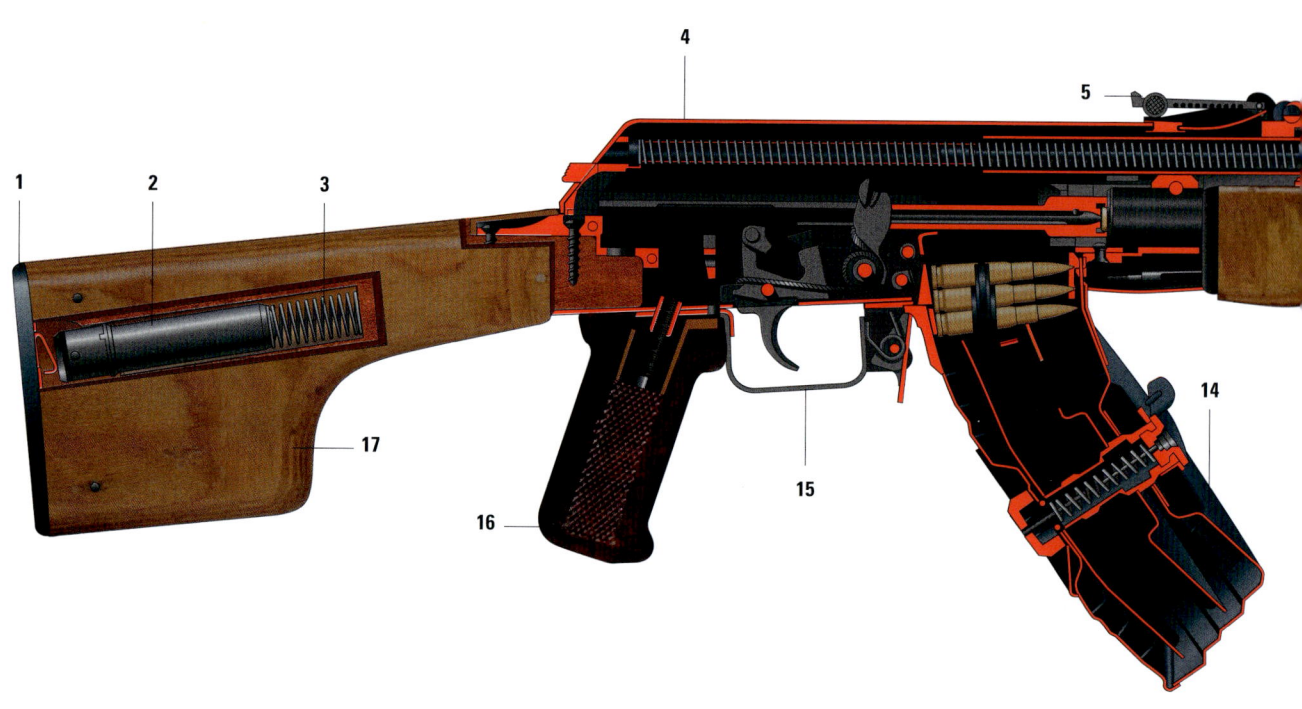

An RPK-16 with 95-round drum magazine and suppressor. The weapon's large buttstock and suppressor enable better control when firing bursts. (Vitaly V. Kuzmin/Wikimedia/CC BY-SA 4.0)

An RPKN fitted with an NPS-3 optical sight. (Insurgentleman/Wikimedia/CC BY-SA 4.0)

Although NATO armies adopted squad automatic weapons for the 5.56×45mm cartridge such as the FN Minimi, which were not based on the standard infantry rifles of these armies, there were a couple of NATO/SEATO armies that did issue rifle-based LMGs: Australia, with the AUG-HB; and Britain, with the L86A2 Light Support Weapon. As a matter of interest, the US M249 will take a Standardization Agreement (STANAG) magazine (M16-compatible), though in the author's experience, this is an inefficient use of the M249.

THE PK

As mentioned previously, the Soviet Union's military leadership had been impressed by the GPMG concept embodied in the German MG 34 and MG 42. The RPD had offered an appealing squad automatic weapon, one that was chambered for the intermediate 7.62×39mm cartridge, but its lack of range and penetration, as well as its propensity to overheat in sustained fire, limited its effectiveness.

One potential replacement was the Nikitin-Sokolov PN1 machine gun of the mid-1950s, which offered a weapon chambered for the 7.62×54mmR cartridge, incorporated an air-cooled quick-change barrel, was belt-fed, and had a self-regulating gas system. As of 1958, 500–1,000 of these weapons had been produced for field trials. Development was derailed, however, by another machine gun designed by Kalashnikov. Designated the PK (*Pulemyot Kalashnikova*; "Kalashnikov's machine gun"), testing confirmed it be a viable GPMG and it was adopted in 1961. Because the RPD had proven unsatisfactory for various reasons, including its somewhat anemic chambering for a GPMG, the PK returned to the long-serving 7.62×54mmR cartridge.

An array of versions would enter service: the bipod-mounted PK, for use as an LMG; the PKS tripod-mounted MMG or GPMG; the PKT tank-mounted machine gun; and the PKB armored personnel carrier-mounted machine gun (Popenker & Williams 2008: 241–42). It is noteworthy that the heavy, non-fluted barrel of the PKT is longer than that of the PK so that ballistics were similar to those of the SGMT, which it replaced. This was practical as it meant that it was not necessary to replace the expensive tank sights (Popenker & Williams 2008: 261).

The PK is air-cooled and may only be fired on full-auto. It fires from an open bolt, which helps avoid "cook-offs." It employs a gas-operated,

BELOW LEFT
A look under the top cover of a PKM shows the "claw" that grabs a cartridge from the ammunition belt and also the barrel lock pushed to the left side to allow quick change of the barrel. (Author)

BELOW RIGHT
A Finnish PKM, June 2014. (MKFI/Wikimedia/Public Domain)

THE PKM REVEALED

7.62mm PKM machine gun

1. Buttplate
2. Skeleton buttstock
3. Barrel-change grip
4. Barrel
5. Front sight
6. Flash suppressor
7. Gas tube
8. Gas piston
9. Bipod (cleaning rod inside strut)
10. Trigger guard
11. Pistol grip
12. Cleaning-kit spring
13. Cleaning kit
14. Rear sight
15. Top cover and feed assembly
16. Claw feed
17. Firing pin
18. Round in chamber
19. Recoil spring

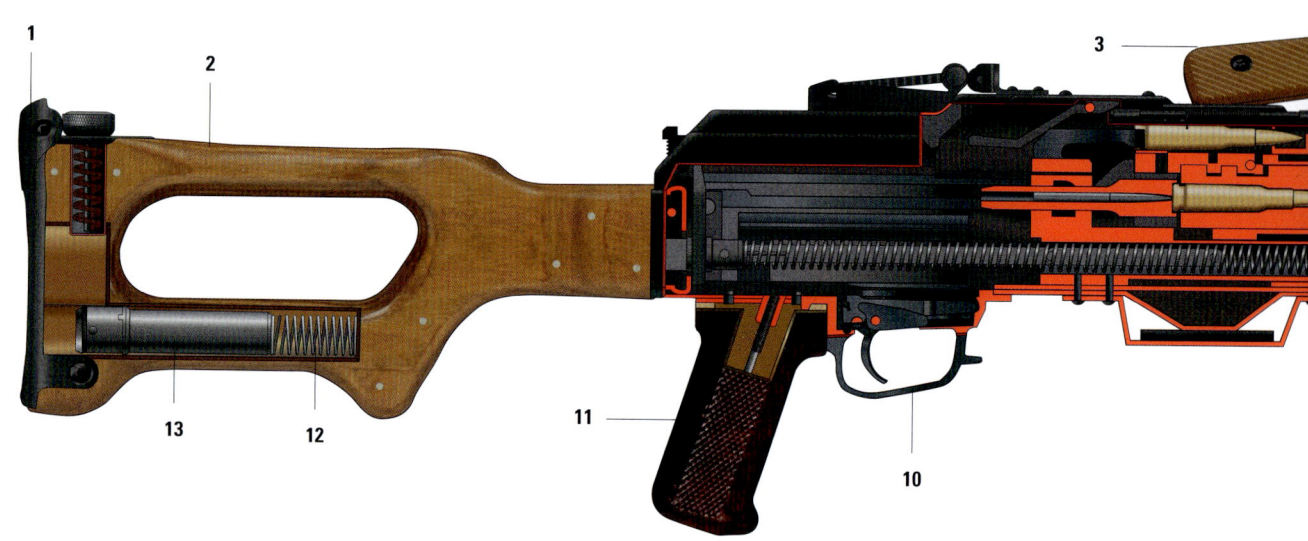

Pictured in 2018, an Iraqi soldier demonstrates the procedure for raising the top cover of a PK variant to load or unload an ammunition belt; in this case the links are empty of rounds. (DVIDS/Public Domain)

long-stroke piston operating system below the barrel (unlike typical Kalashnikov designs, which position the gas system above the barrel) with a rotating bolt. Because of the chambering for the 7.62×54mmR cartridge, the PK incorporates a two-stage belt feed from steel non-disintegrating ammunition belts. A manual gas regulator enhances reliability when firing continuously or in adverse conditions. Another feature of the PK that allows better, sustained fire is its quick-change barrel. The wooden skeleton buttstock allows very comfortable firing from the prone position.

The PK/PKS continued in use with Soviet forces until 1969, after which the improved PKM/PKMS entered service. The PKM is another design that has been widely deployed, and in some cases built, in former Warsaw Pact and client states. An indication of the popularity and durability of the PK line of machine guns is that more than 1 million have been manufactured.

Combat in Afghanistan between 1979 and 1989 revealed the need for a heavier weapon capable of firing the 7.62×54mmR cartridge rather than the RPK's 7.62×39mm and the RPK-74's 5.45×39mm. Combat in the mountains, however, where the weapon would be carried by airmobile and airborne troops on patrols, resulted in a PKM variant better designed for counterinsurgency warfare. This was the Pecheneg, a PKM without the quick-change barrel but with an integral bipod.

When compared to the RPK-74 in use as a section support weapon, the Pecheneg proved particularly useful during operations in Chechnya where the 7.62×54mmR chambering gave longer range during mountainous operations as well as better penetration of barriers in urban operations (Popenker & Williams 2008: 244).

The Pecheneg had a heavier barrel with cooling fins and a forced-air barrel-cooling jacket to allow more sustained fire. Other features included an improved flash hider and a carry handle. It was claimed that the Pecheneg could fire up to 600 rounds in continuous fire without barrel damage (Popenker & Williams 2008: 62). Belts of 100, 200, and 250 rounds were available for both the PKM and Pecheneg.

A Pecheneg on display in October 2011. (Vitaly V. Kuzmin/Wikimedia/CC BY-SA 4.0)

There was another iteration of the PKM designed for more portability, the AEK-999 *Barsuk* (Badger) GPMG. Also based on the PKM, the AEK-999 was developed at the Kovrov Mechanical Plant. The weapon retained the basic PKM receiver, but employed a barrel of fabricated steel normally used for aircraft machine guns. This barrel was fluted to lighten it and also to aid cooling, as it did not allow for quick changing. Still, the AEK-999's barrel was intended to allow continuous fire without the need for a barrel change. As the AEK-999 was intended to allow firing from the hip, it had a polymer forearm, a more effective muzzle brake, and a bipod mounted farther forward on the barrel. It was also designed to take a suppressor. The AEK-999 could also be mounted on the PKM tripod and take the same 100-round ammunition belts. Limited numbers of the AEK-999 were acquired by OMON (MVD special forces), but it was the Pecheneg that was adopted by most Russian troops and saw far more use in combat, especially with elite infantry such as the airborne and airmobile forces (Popenker & Williams 2008: 244–45).

Other developments of the PK included the PKN and PKSN with rails for optical sights. The PKZ, which may never progress beyond prototype stage, uses only a collimator sight.

A Pecheneg-SP in August 2014. This variant features a suppressor for noiseless and flameless fire. (Vitaly V. Kuzmin/Wikimedia/CC BY-SA 4.0)

THE NSV

Though the KPV and DShKM remained in use, the need for an HMG that could be used more readily for infantry support indicated the requirement for a more mobile weapon. Development of a new HMG to meet this need began in 1969 with three designers – G.I. Nikitin, Y.M. Sokolov, and V.I. Volkov – contributing, hence the designation of the weapon as the "NSV." Introduced into Soviet service in 1971, the NSV was also known colloquially among troops as the *Utyos* (rock or cliff) (Popenker & Williams 2008: 243).

Chambered for the 12.7×108mm cartridge, the NSV is lighter (25kg) than the DShKM (34kg), and is readily mounted on a tripod. It is a versatile weapon and can serve in the antiaircraft role, or for vehicle or shipboard mounting. Its action is gas-operated, employing a gas chamber with a three-position gas regulator and a long-stroke gas piston. A bolt carrier is in rollers, with a spring buffer for the bolt group being located in the rear of the receiver. The weapon is air-cooled and has a quick-detachable barrel. It is recommended that a pause in firing or a barrel change take place after 100 rounds of continuous fire. The NSV fires from an open bolt and is capable only of full-auto fire. A non-disintegrating ammunition belt is used to feed the weapon. For ease of transport, the feed belts are assembled from ten-round sections. Standard belt feed is from right to left, but the weapon can be configured for left to right feed if necessary. Cartridges are pushed down from the belt onto the feed tray. Of special note is the NSV's breechblock, which employs three side-folding linked sub-blocks, all in line for locking and firing; the recoil after firing allows the blocks to fall out of line to eject an empty case and chamber a new one.

An NSV-12.7 in Finnish service, June 2013. (MKFI/Public Domain)

An NSV. (Vitaly V. Kuzmin/Wikimedia/CC BY-SA 4.0)

To give an idea of the enhanced portability of the NSV, when tripod mounted with a 50-round belt, the weapon weighs 100kg less than the DShKM on a wheeled mount with the same 50-round belt. Crew for the NSV consists of two soldiers, one of whom can carry the infantry tripod. Total weight with optical sight and tripod is 43kg, with overall length when mounted on the tripod being 1,900mm. Rate of fire is 700–800rd/min.

The NSV was also more accurate and could be fabricated using more modern techniques (i.e. its receiver was a steel stamping). Among the aids to accuracy on the updated NSVP version were a muzzle brake with multiple ports that reduced recoil and a better-balanced tripod. An optical sight designated the SPP in either 3× or 6× was another aid to accuracy.

Although suitable for infantry use, the NSV also replaced the DShKM on many tanks and was used as an infantry antiaircraft weapon. Unlike most machine guns, the fire controls for the NSV are built into the mount, with a solenoid control available for those weapons mounted on tanks. When mounted on a ground-based tripod, the weapon was designated the NSV-12.7 or NSV N3; when fitted with a night optic it was designated the NSV-12.7 N4; and on an armored vehicle coaxial mount it was designated the NSVT.

According to Russian weapons expert Maxim Popenker, after the dissolution of the Soviet Union, the NSV production facility was located in the newly independent Kazakhstan. As a result, development work began on a new HMG to be manufactured in Russia, resulting in the Kord (Popenker & Williams 2008: 256).

THE KORD

A Russian design team worked on an improved 12.7×108mm HMG from 1987, though the weapon did not enter service until 1998. Designated the KORD (*Kovrovskiye Oruzheyniki Degtyarovtsy*; "Kovrov gunsmiths Degtyaryov'"), the new HMG also had the official Russian designation 6P50. Its designers were D.S. Lipsman, A.A. Namitulin, N.M. Obidin, and V.I. Zhiryokin. The Kord was manufactured at the V.A. Degtyaryov Plant at Kovrov.

The Kord seems to have been used primarily by troops of the MVD (Ministry of Internal Affairs). Various mechanical changes reduced recoil, through use of a hydraulic buffer in the stock, thus allowing better control on full-auto. The Kord is also more accurate than the DShK. Considering the internal-security role of the MVD, this offers a tactical advantage.

The Kord is gas-operated, employing a long-stroke gas piston located below the barrel and a rotary bolt. It is air-cooled and can be fired on full-auto only. The major functional difference from the NSV is elimination of the pivoting breechblock, which was replaced with a rotating bolt. The quick-detachable barrel is fitted with a muzzle brake – cylindrical on early production examples, and flat on later production weapons. Ammunition belts of the same type as used for the NSV are used; standard feed is from right to left, but this can be switched if desired. Fired cartridge cases are normally ejected forward. The mounting interface is the same as that of the NSV, and as with the NSV, fire controls are located on the mount. A siderail on the left of the receiver allows quick mounting of optical sights.

Variants of the Kord include the 6P49 (standard), the 6P50 (infantry version, 1,580mm overall and 25kg), the 6P50-1 (infantry version mounted on a bipod; overall length 1,980mm and 32kg; bipod allows traverse of 15 degrees right or left), the 6P50-2 (mounted on 6T19 tripod; length still 1,980mm but weight is 52kg), the 6P50-3 (infantry version on 6U6 multipurpose mount; 75kg weight, same overall length, ejection to the right; generally mounted on watercraft), and the 6P51 (coaxial version with left-hand feed). There is also the 6C21 remote weapon station that can be used with either the Kord or the PKMT. For tank mounting, the T-72B3 version of the Kord may be used. To facilitate export sales the Kord is also available chambered for the 12.7×99mm (.50-caliber Browning Machine Gun) cartridge.

Ukrainian soldiers of the Azov Brigade practice with a captured Kord, November 2023. Owing to its light recoil, the Kord can not only be mounted on the NSV's tripod but also on a bipod. When bipod-mounted, the weight is only 31kg for the Kord, which not only became the standard infantry HMG but also the coaxial weapon on Russian main battle tanks such as the T-80U and T-90; it may also be retrofitted to older main battle tanks such as the T-64 and T-72. For both infantry and armored-vehicle deployment, the Kord has proven to offer excellent accuracy out to 2,000m. The Kord also offers enhanced accuracy when firing longer bursts – especially important in combat. (Sipa US/Alamy Stock Photo)

An RPL-20 in August 2020. (Vitaly V. Kuzmin/Wikimedia/ CC BY-SA 4.0)

THE RPL-20

Development of a new LMG by Kalashnikov Concern intended for Russian special-forces use has continued, with a prototype unveiled in 2020. Designated the RPL-20 (*Ruchnoy Pulyemot Lentochnyy*; "belt-fed machine gun"), this weapon is chambered for the 5.45×39mm cartridge, but is belt-fed, unlike the AK-74 and RPK-74, which are box magazine-fed. Details of the operating system have not been forthcoming at the time of writing, in part to avoid copying. The basic features are known, however, including firing from an open bolt and feeding from a box holding 100 rounds of 5.45×39mm cartridges. During the design process a dual-feed option to allow use of either a box magazine or ammunition belts was considered, but rejected. The RPL-20 weighs 5.2kg, which is 2.0kg lighter than the FN Minimi, its NATO equivalent. Its changeable barrel is available in two lengths, the shorter one presumably for airborne/special-operations usage. (Litovkin 2020).

Russian weapons designers have also been cognizant of the US Next Generation Squad Weapon Program, which would replace the M4 Carbine, M249 SAW, and M240 GPMG with new weapons chambered for the common 6.8mm cartridge. As a result there has been ongoing experimentation with a Russian 6.02×41mm cartridge for rifles and machine guns. Weapons tested reportedly include PKM-based machine guns as well as the AN-94 assault rifle (Anonymous 2019).

An RPL-20 on display in 2020. (CAPTCHA332/Wikimedia/ CC BY-SA 4.0)

USE
A universal battlefield presence

A Syrian soldier in NBC gear and armed with a PKM, pictured during a firepower demonstration in Operation *Desert Shield*, May 1992. (Technical Sergeant H.H. Deffner/Wikimedia/Public Domain)

Some of the machine guns used by the Soviet Union in the post-1945 era first saw service during World War II and even before. For example, the DShK-38 entered Red Army service in 1938, with 9,000 being produced during World War II. That early usage falls outside the remit of this work, however, but the DShK's postwar combat history is discussed below.

Although the RPD, chambered for the new 7.62×39mm cartridge, was in limited production during the final years of World War II, it was not officially adopted until 1948, and it was not until 1953 that it reached Soviet troops in substantial numbers. From the 1960s until the present day, the RPD has been used by insurgents and by many Developing World countries, and as the United States and its allies have faced proxies of China, Russia, Iran, and other states, they have also faced the RPD.

Close-up of the RPD's cocking handle, which allows good leverage for chambering a round. (Author)

The RPD's "club foot" buttstock aids in grasping tightly against the shoulder with the support hand while firing. (Author)

INDOCHINA TO ALGERIA

The DShK/DShkM was an effective weapon for Communist forces during the Chinese Civil War (1927–49). A claim was reportedly made by the Chinese Communists that in August 1945, they received 300,000 rifles and 4,800 machine guns from the Soviet Union. In the early 1950s, China obtained a production license and tooling from the Soviet Union to produce the DShKM, which the Chinese designated the Type 54. It would be mounted on Chinese vehicles until almost the end of the 20th century.

The First Indochina War (1946–54) saw French forces in combat against the Viet Minh and other Communist groups in Indochina. As with many insurgent groups, the Viet Minh used an assortment of captured weapons, many acquired by the French from the United States, as well as weapons from the Soviet Union, including the DShK/DShKM. Perhaps the most noteworthy use of the DShKM was during the battle of Dien Bien Phu (March 13–May 7, 1954), when approximately 100 DShKMs and 80 37mm antiaircraft guns were deployed in the hills surrounding the French base, seeking to bring down aircraft dropping supplies to the besieged garrison. As a result, the French lost 62 aircraft and another 180 were damaged (Roblin 2021).

As the siege progressed, fewer landing strips and drop zones were available to the French, allowing Viet Minh machine-gunners to pre-zero their DShKMs on the paths the slow-moving transport aircraft had to take. Not only aircraft flying supply missions were attacked but also those attempting to drop paratroopers to reinforce the defenders. The DShKMs along with the 37mm antiaircraft guns proved one of the deciding factors in the Viet Minh's victory at Dien Bien Phu.

Although the author has seen vague references to RPDs being captured during the Korean War (1950–53), if any were, they would likely have been only prototypes supplied by the Chinese for field testing prior to the Chinese People's Liberation Army's adoption of the Type 56, the domestically produced version of the RPD.

In service with the Chinese and the North Koreans, the DShK/DShKM saw service during the Korean War in both the antiaircraft and antivehicle roles. At the beginning of the Korean War, the Chinese People's Volunteer Army (PVA) used an array of machine guns: both US weapons (including the .50-caliber M2 HMG) captured from the Chinese Nationalist Army and weapons provided by the Soviet Union. During the initial crossing of the Yalu River, captured Japanese 13.2mm machine guns were also employed. (Anonymous 2021). Once the Soviet-made DShKM arrived when Chinese forces intervened in Korea, it saw widespread use providing antiaircraft coverage for Chinese troops. Although the Chinese found the DShKM reliable and easy to operate, they discovered that difficulty experienced in moving the weapon on its wheeled mount was a disadvantage when advancing against United Nations Command forces with their supporting air power. For improved mobility, the Chinese tried mounting the DShKM on trucks, but US air power inhibited the trucks' movement during daylight hours (Anonymous 2021).

At the beginning of the Korean War, the Korean People's Army had 400 T-34-85 medium tanks and SU-76M self-propelled guns, most of which were subsequently lost to US armor or aircraft. When the PVA entered the war, they supplied some Type 58 medium tanks, their designation for the Chinese-produced T-34-85. The Type 58 tanks were still armed with 7.62×54mmR machine guns such as the DT, however. It was not until the introduction of the T-54/T-55 main battle tank that the DShKM became standard on Soviet tanks in service with the Chinese.

By the mid-1950s, as the SKS and later the AK-47 came to be widely distributed to Soviet client states, the RPD, which was chambered for the same 7.62×39mm round, was used in combat in Communist insurgencies and other conflicts.

One of the first times NATO forces faced the RPD was during the Suez Crisis (October 29–November 7, 1956) when Soviet-supplied RPDs were used by Egyptian forces in combat against British, French, and Israeli forces. During the 1950s, Egypt also began producing RPDs, but it is unclear how many of those had reached Egyptian troops by the time of the Suez Crisis. Egypt also received DShKMs from the Soviet Union, some of which may have seen action against helicopters used by Britain's Royal Marine Commandos conducting airmobile operations.

Urban counterinsurgency, Hungary, 1956 (opposite)

During the Hungarian Revolution (October 23–November 4, 1956), Soviet troops moved quickly to control the streets. The deployment of armored vehicles and machine guns served as an implied threat as well as a deadly reality to control the streets of Budapest and other urban areas. Thousands of Hungarians were killed or wounded. In reality, the "revolutionary militias" formed by students and others dissidents stood little chance against the State Protection Authority (Hungarian secret police) backed by Soviet troops. Estimates were that around 2,500 Hungarians and 700 Soviet troops were killed, with many more wounded.

Here amid the destruction, a BTR-40 armored personnel carrier of a motor-rifle unit has been deployed to control an intersection. The gunner on the vehicle has manned its 7.62×51mm SGMB MMG. A dismounted light-machine-gunner covers the flank with a 7.62×39mm RPD LMG, while the rear of the BTR-40 is covered by a pair of troops armed with AK-47 assault rifles.

FIRING THE RPD

The combinations of the "club foot" buttstock, pistol grip, foregrip, and bipod aided the RPD gunner in engaging the enemy effectively. Although a fit gunner could fire the RPD from the shoulder, it should be noted that the foregrip is rather small and the gunner's hand can get burned from contact with the barrel if care is not taken.

The loading drill for the RPD is relatively simple. First, two 50-round linked sections have the cartridges pressed into them from the top until the rims of the cartridges are snapped into place. Once the two sections are loaded, they are joined by mating the tongue of the end link to the starting link of the other. When the first section is empty it will fall free.

The belt is then rolled tightly and fitted into the drum. With the tab of the belt protruding the drum is slid onto the RPD's receiver, then locked in place. Next, the cocking handle is pulled to the rear to lock the bolt back. Then, the top cover is lifted and the linked belt is carefully placed next to the stop; the cover is then closed. When the bolt is back, care must be taken not to touch the trigger. The safety may be applied if immediate engagement is not planned.

The author firing the RPD from the prone position offers an example of how low the gunner can position himself even with the drum in place; note the ejection of cartridges to the right. (Author)

RPDs from Egypt also found their way to the *Front de liberation nationale* during the Algerian War (1954–62), although Egypt primarily supplied Bren guns (Bouzid 1996). Especially in the insurgencies of the 1950s and 1960s, the RPD proved popular due to its portability and its chambering for the ubiquitous 7.62×39mm round.

THE VIETNAM WAR

For the US armed forces, the first large-scale encounter with the RPD was during the Vietnam War. Although the DPM had been in use by the PAVN and VC, as of April 1964, when US troops first encountered PAVN regulars, RPDs were in use (Guttman 2019). The RPDs encountered by US troops were normally the Chinese Type 56 version, though some Soviet-manufactured RPDs were also noted.

In combat, the RPD proved to have a shorter range than the DP-27 and other machine guns chambered for a full-power rifle cartridge. The Soviet military seemed to view the RPD as a short- to medium-range weapon, however. Although the fixed barrel was a disadvantage, Soviet Army gunners were trained to fire short bursts and were, in fact, only issued 300 rounds as the RPD's standard combat load.

During active operations, the RPD's lightweight bipod proved fragile. Another disadvantage for movement at night was that the drum magazine was a carrier and not a feed device. As a result, the belted cartridges rattled. Some problems arose with early-production RPDs that were later fixed. For example, on the original RPD ammunition belt, a cartridge could work its way out of the tab, causing a malfunction. Early-production RPDs also lacked folding dust covers for the ports, allowing foreign matter to enter the weapon.

Ergonomically, the RPD has some positive features. The author has found the stock conducive to excellent control when firing on full-auto while in the prone position. A foregrip helps in picking up the RPD to move it between firing positions and aids a strong and skilled gunner in firing from the shoulder while moving. The bipod, though not especially sturdy, also aids in full-automatic fire from the prone position. Light enough to fire from the hip or even from the shoulder, the RPD's weight (7.4kg empty) is not prohibitive. Because of the use of the intermediate 7.62×39mm round, recoil even on full-automatic is barely noticeable when firing bursts from the prone position. Note that because of the trajectory of the 7.62×39mm round, the use of tracer ammunition is desirable to get rounds on target. Note also that the rear sight is marked to 1,000m – but that is optimistic!

As the RPD only fires on full-automatic, trigger control is necessary to keep bursts short. As the barrel is not of the quick-change type, controlled bursts are necessary to prevent the barrel overheating. The fact that the RPD fires from an open bolt helps avoid rounds "cooking off" (firing without pulling the trigger due to a hot chamber).

As with the AK-47, sight adjustments for elevation and windage are made to the RPD's front post sight. Belt feed for the RPD is from the left side; it takes a bit of practice to thread it properly, but the feed is normally reliable. The selector/safety lever is located on the right side of the receiver above the pistol grip. It is small and relatively easy to operate. The cocking handle is located forward of the trigger guard on the right side and is large enough to allow easy use, though it requires moving the right hand from the firing position to cock.

In evaluating the RPD it is necessary to consider the NATO weapons that would have been its equivalent during its lifespan. During the first decades of the RPD's service, the venerable US Browning Automatic Rifle (BAR) would have been its closest rival. The advantages of the RPD at that time were its use of an intermediate service cartridge and its ability to take belted ammunition, allowing more sustained fire. The BAR was limited to 20-round box magazines and fired the powerful .30-06 cartridge, which gave it more range and striking power. Perhaps a better comparison would be with the British Bren gun, which was chambered for the .303 full-power cartridge. Though the Bren took box magazines they were of 30-round capacity. By 1980, when the FN Minimi, which also chambered an intermediate cartridge (5.56×45mm), had begun to enter service, the RPD had been replaced as a front-line weapon for Russia and other Warsaw Pact armies, though it has remained in use with many insurgent groups.

A Type 50 or Type 57 MMG (the Chinese versions of the SG-43 and SGM, respectively) in North Vietnamese hands in September 1967. Aid from the Soviet Union included tooling and blueprints to produce these machine guns. (Underwood Archives, Inc/Alamy Stock Photo)

US Special Forces faced the RPD in battle and turned captured examples against the enemy. For example, Vietnam Special Operations Group commander Henry L. (Dick) Thompson faced the RPD in the hands of PAVN troops during cross-border operations into North Vietnam and found that when discovered by the PAVN the Americans faced a combination of AK-47, RPD, and RPG fire at close range while attempting to escape and evade to reach an LZ (Landing Zone) for a "hot" extraction (Thompson 2023: 96).

For Military Assistance Command Vietnam Special Operations Group (MACV-SOG) operators, the RPD proved highly useful on clandestine missions when they were using ComBloc weapons such as the AK-47. Not only did the RPD take the same ammunition and have the same sound when fired as the RPDs in use with PAVN and VC forces, it could be altered for easier carriage on these missions. Tactically, SOG teams used the "chopped" (shortened) RPD as an ambush or counter-ambush weapon rather than a fire-support weapon. Modifications included shortening the barrel and buttstock to cut the weapon's overall length to 31in (78.7cm). This also reduced the weapon's weight to approximately 5.4kg. Other changes included modifying the ammunition belt to take 125 rounds, rather than 100 rounds. As remaining silent for clandestine cross-border insertions was paramount, a slice of linoleum was placed in the drum to counter rattle (Plaster 2020). The "chopped" RPD was substantially lighter and shorter than the US M60 GPMG (10.5kg and 1,105mm overall), took 7.62×39mm cartridges, and sounded different to a US machine gun. US SOG did not normally have access to the Stoner 63 LMG (5.3kg and 1,022mm overall), but SOG teams did also use "chopped" M60s.

Normally, SOG teams did not use captured 7.62×39mm ammunition because of fear that it might consist of "Eldest Son" rounds (Thompson 2023: 191), 7.62×39mm cartridges that had been rigged by US personnel to explode when fired. These were placed in VC arms caches that had

Troops of the US 5th Marines with an RPD (left) and an AK-47, near Da Nang, Vietnam, early 1969. Most US troops did not receive foreign-weapons training at this time, and care had to be taken to avoid negligent discharges. (USMC Archives/Wikimedia/CC BY 2.0)

Con Thien, South Vietnam, January 1969: US Marines of the 3d Reconnaissance Battalion carry a captured DShKM, identifiable by its flash hider and fluted barrel. The Chinese copy of the DShK, the Type 54, does not have a fluted barrel. (Corporal Bob Partain/Wikimedia/Public Domain)

been discovered but not destroyed. SOG teams often carried one or more AK-47 magazines that had been so altered in case they found an arms cache. "Eldest Son" was a psychological-operations mission designed to make the North Vietnamese forces distrust their weapons. Other types of ammunition, such as 12.7×108mm rounds for the DShKM and 82mm Type 67 mortar rounds, were also booby-trapped.

In combat, the PAVN, VC, and US special-operations troops found the RPD had three major weaknesses. First, when long, sustained bursts were fired, it tended to jam. Second, as the RPD did not have a removable barrel, it tended to overheat if the gunner fired more than 100–150 rounds in a minute. Third, gunners found that at ranges beyond 250–300m the RPD was inaccurate.

A fourth problem found was that the RPD's cartridges would rattle around in the box magazine when moving, thus alerting the enemy to the presence of enemy forces. Prior to firing, users of the RPD also found that it was necessary to open the drum and check that the notch on each link had been securely snapped into the cartridge's extraction groove and that the loaded ammunition belt had been carefully rolled to fit the drum. PAVN troops found ways to counter these shortcomings, however. Exercising fire discipline lessened the RPD's tendency to jam and alleviated overheating. As the tactical environment in Vietnam kept most engagements to ranges under 200m, the longer-range accuracy issue was less significant.

Also used in substantial numbers by the PAVN and VC, the RPK (chambered for the same 7.62×39mm cartridge) was lighter and more portable than the RPD. Additionally, the RPK's box magazines did not rattle, as did the belt in the box of the RPD. (It should be pointed out that 75-round drums were available for the RPK, but do not seem to have been used in any great quantity by the VC.) The RPK had first been observed at the 1966 May Day parade in Moscow, so it would have reached the hands of the PAVN/VC about the time of the major US troop buildup.

Later in the Vietnam War, c.1970, the PAVN used its own copy of the hybrid LMG, the TUL-1, which combined a Chinese Type 56 receiver with an RPK stock and RPD sights. After the Vietnam War ended in April 1975, the reunified Vietnam obtained the rights to produce the RPK and, thus, no longer needed the TUL-1. Nevertheless, the RPD remained in PAVN and VC use. (Guttman 2019).

A noteworthy aspect of the VC's use of the RPD and RPK occurred during the employment of "hugging" tactics against US and ARVN infantry. By getting as close to the enemy units as possible – "hugging" them – the VC made it difficult for US troops to call in fire support from artillery or helicopter gunships. Because the RPD and RPK were light and could be quickly repositioned, both weapons lent themselves to such tactics.

Helicopters gave US troops an edge in terms of mobility and aerial fire support, thus making them prime targets for the PAVN and VC. Prior to 1966, the insurgents primarily attempted to engage helicopters with AK-47 or SKS rifles; in that year, however, DShKM HMGs began to arrive for use by the VC. Emplaced DShKMs positioned around potential LZs or in other areas that were overflown accounted for a substantial number of the more than 5,600 US helicopters lost during the Vietnam War.

When using the RPD or RPK from entrenched positions, VC forces normally shaped their front lines in an "L," "U," or "V" position. These are fairly standard ambush positions and have the advantage of enhancing interlocking fields of fire, but care must be taken with the "U" and "V" positions to avoid friendly fire. Bunkers were often positioned just behind the front lines so that the guerrillas could retreat from US artillery fire, then reoccupy their front line to engage US troops with machine guns. Another VC tactic was what was termed the "fishing tactic," in which the guerrillas would encircle a US position in order to lure reinforcements, which would theoretically be attrited by VC machine-gun and mortar fire.

THE SOVIET–AFGHAN WAR

The first major use of the last generation of Soviet machine guns took place in Afghanistan. In fact, both sides were armed with some of the same weapons, though those in Mujahideen hands were often Chinese copies.

Dating from 1984, the US Army publication FM 100-2-1 *The Soviet Army: Operations and Tactics* gives some idea of the place of machine guns in various Soviet Army units during the Soviet–Afghan War (1979–89). A motor-rifle battalion was equipped with nine PKMs and 27 RPK-74s. For comparison, an airborne company equipped with BMD infantry fighting vehicles was issued nine RPK-74s. In addition, each BMD carried one 73mm 2A28 semiautomatic gun, and one coaxial and two hull-mounted PKTs. With up to 14 BMDs that gave an airborne company, which might be fighting behind enemy lines, a lot of firepower.

Soviet forces used the 7.62×54mmR RPK initially as a squad automatic weapon, to be replaced by the 5.45×39mm RPK-74 when the AK-74

A captured RPD in Afghan hands in October 1980. (Hiromi Nagakura/Alamy Stock Photo)

entered service. Most important for the Mujahideen was the availability of the 12.7×108mm DShKM and 14.5×114mm KPV, which could be positioned on the heights to interdict Soviet convoys and also to down helicopters. Often the DShKMs were positioned in caves where they were somewhat protected from Soviet helicopter gunships. Another Mujahideen tactic proved relatively effective against Soviet airmobile troops being landed by helicopter. As the assault force was being inserted, the Mujahideen would launch an ambush on the LZ with mass LMG and RPG fire, followed up with an assault to overrun the disorganized landing force.

Afghan ambush, c.1985 (previous pages)

Soviet airmobile and other troops made extensive use of helicopters to insert on high ground to interdict the Mujahideen from attacking convoys passing through valleys. Here, an Mi-8 has just inserted infantryman, but they have come under attack from an Afghan guerrilla using a 12.7×108mm DShKM HMG from higher ground. The DShKM was most likely used to engage the helicopter during the insertion but also proved deadly for some of the troops disembarking from the helicopter. Beginning in 1986, US-supplied Stinger infrared-homing surface-to-air missiles proved lethal against Soviet helicopters in the mountains.

A Soviet marksman armed with an SVD Dragunov rifle has already been killed before attempting to neutralize the threat. The soldier at left is engaging the Mujahideen gunner with an RPK-74 LMG. Farther to the right, a PKM GPMG gunner and his assistant are preparing to engage. The PKM's 7.62×54mmR ammunition will give greater range than the RPK-74's 7.62×39mm cartridge, allowing more effective counterfire against the DShKM.

Soviet infantry units were armed with the RPK and PKM. Range limitations of the RPK were addressed in Soviet infantry doctrine c.1978, which held that when on the defense, machine-gun fire would be withheld until the enemy was within 400m. It should be noted that this doctrine had been developed on the assumption of war against NATO forces on the North German Plain (Department of the Army 1978: 4-10). For mobile antiaircraft protection, vehicle-mounted machine guns such as the DShKM or KPV would be deployed to give 360-degree coverage while retaining the ability to rejoin the column quickly (Department of the Army 1978: 5-28). As the Mujahideen lacked air power, however, these vehicles were deployed to cover the heights during road movement.

Despite its shortcomings in terms of range and sustained fire, the RPK proved relatively effective in Afghanistan, having superior reliability and the capability to use either the 40-round (or 30-round AK-47) box magazine or the 75-round drum magazine. The tendency of ammunition in the drum magazine to rattle has been noted previously. Box magazines were easier to carry in magazine pouches. The 40-round box magazine was also easier to load. It was estimated that the typical RPK gunner could fire five or six 40-round box magazines in the time it took to load one 75-round drum (Besedovskyy 2023b).

The RPK-74 and RPKS-74 saw extensive use once they became available c.1980. The normal estimate of these weapons' effective range when used by an experienced gunner was 500m. Seeing substantial use with airborne/airmobile troops and *spetsnaz*, the RPKS-74 had the disadvantage of a very stiff button release for the stock. Troops learned to use either a bullet tip or other thin tool to release the stock, however (Besedovskyy 2023b).

The PKM served as the primary MMG for Soviet forces throughout the Soviet–Afghan War. Early in the conflict, however, second-line troops from Turkmenistan Military District that took part in the original invasion were still armed with PKs. An advantage of the PKM was its ability to inflict significant casualties on the enemy. According to Isby (1988: 303), a PKM

An Afghan fighter with a PKM, 1989. (Kees Metselaar/Alamy Stock Photo)

has a 50 percent chance of hitting a standing enemy soldier at 550m with a 6–9-round burst. As with other machine guns, the PKM had a greater chance of inflicting multiple enemy casualties when firing from an enfilading position. At 50m the probability of hits against an immobile enemy was 97 percent and at 100m 83 percent, but against a moving enemy at 550m, the burst size probability drops to 40 percent. The PKMS had the advantage of weighing only 12kg with gun and Stepanov 6T5 tripod. This compares favorably with the NATO-standard FN MAG with tripod, at 21kg.

There were pros and cons to the PKM's 7.62×54mmR chambering. An advantage of the use of a battle rifle-caliber cartridge was greater penetration – 37mm on mild steel or 127mm on concrete (Isby 1988: 304). The downside, however, was that two calibers of ammunition (7.62×39mm and 7.62×54mmR) had to be carried. This same problem would arise with NATO armies in which the M4 or other assault rifles would be chambered in 5.56×45mm and the FN MAG/M240 would be chambered for the 7.62×51mm cartridge. In the Soviet Army, the RPK chambered the same cartridge as the AK-47, thus easing logistics for the squad. Likewise in NATO armies the FN Minimi/M249 was chambered for the 5.56×45mm cartridge; hence its designation as a "squad automatic weapon."

As with many armies, Soviet doctrine was that when in a defensive position at night, the machine guns would be positioned so that their fields of fire covered a fixed area, often delineated by stakes to control the pivoting arc of the weapon's barrel (Isby 1988: 305).

Early in the Soviet–Afghan War the RPK was used as the squad automatic weapon, but once the AK-74 became the standard infantry rifle, the RPK was replaced with the RPK-74 for uniformity of ammunition. Motor-rifle troops normally were equipped with the PKM, but it was considered heavy for dismounted troops, especially in the broken terrain in Afghanistan. If used by dismounted troops, the PKM was equipped with either a bipod or tripod. HMGs such as the DShK, NSV, and KPVT were used against enemy troops at ranges up to 2,000m and/or behind cover that could be penetrated only by the more powerful 12.7×108mm or 14.5×114mm ammunition (Russian General Staff 2002: 39). It should be noted that Soviet doctrine was that suppression of enemy small-arms fire took precedence over aimed fire, thus putting great emphasis on the machine gun (Grau & Bartles 2016: 214). The ammunition supply, not all of which was already loaded on belts, could become depleted quickly, however.

One other point should be made: the Soviet Army traditionally included a marksman in each rifle squad. This allowed for more precise long-range fire, which with the SVD semiautomatic rifle could be delivered with more volume than with a bolt-action sniping rifle.

Tank-mounted machine guns (theoretically for air defense) were used against the enemy firing from elevated positions, but doing so exposed the loader to sniper fire through the tank's open hatch. An example of the deployment of machine guns for use in ambushes of the Mujahideen occurred in July 1986, when a 35-man parachute company was equipped with four PKM and four RPKS machine guns and ten MON-100 directional mines, as well as AKMs (Russian General Staff 2002: 206).

As Mujahideen ambushes became more sophisticated, motor-rifle troops normally performed convoy escort duties armed with flamethrowers (presumably the RPO-A *Shmel*) as well as ZSU-23-4 *Shilka* antiaircraft machine guns; helicopter gunships flew overwatch (Russian General Staff 2002: 307).

The Mujahideen also used Soviet or Chinese machine guns. While the RPD had been replaced in most Soviet units, it was widely used by the Mujahideen. Machine guns were seen as prestige items among the Mujahideen and would sometimes be supplied to them to ensure they would take part in a certain operation (Yousaf & Adkin 2001: 103). Mules – always an important mode of transport for Mujahideen machine-gunners – could move out of combat and into and out of Pakistan with weapons, however, as machine guns brought a high price in the Darra gun markets (Yousaf & Adkin 2001: 135).

Training the Mujahideen in tactics for best deployment of the machine guns they possessed was often difficult. For example, advisors from the Pakistani Inter-Services Intelligence attempted to teach the Mujahideen how to "dig in" machine-gun positions and build a trench system leading between emplacements, but found that the Mujahideen did not like to dig. Emplaced 12.7×108mm and 14.5×114mm HMGs served for antiaircraft protection, or were used against light vehicles or infantry. The Mujahideen proved to be effective at emplacing their HMGs in mountainous terrain so that Soviet 14.5×114mm HMGs on BTR-60 armored personnel carriers, which could only be elevated 30 degrees, were ineffective. As a result, by 1983, the Soviets were mounting twin 23mm antiaircraft guns on trucks to counter this tactic (Yousaf & Adkin 2001: 52). Mi-24 helicopter gunships mounting 12.7×108mm HMGs were also effective until Stinger infrared-homing surface-to-air missiles started arriving from the United States in 1986. Another deficiency that arose with the BTR-60-mounted HMGs was that the vehicle was so low care had to be taken, as the barrels had to be elevated sufficiently when firing ahead or to the side to avoid striking friendly troops.

To counter Mujahideen attacks on convoys or advancing ground troops, the Soviets used a combat vehicle or group of vehicles to occupy dominant terrain. Commonly used was the BTR-60, with a main armament of a 14.5×114mm KVT or 12.7×108mm NSV and a secondary coaxial 7.62×54mmR PKT. Normal combat load was 500 rounds for the KVT or NSV and 3,000 rounds for the PKT. Enveloping Soviet airmobile forces sent to cut off the retreat of Mujahideen fighters also relied on crew-served weapons, usually the RPK or PKM. Alternatively, airmobile troops would be committed to attack the Mujahideen from the rear while advancing motor-rifle troops attacked them from the front. Sometimes, one or more NSVs would be used for static overwatch.

A close-up of an NSV's range markings. (Vitaly V. Kuzmin/Wikimedia/CC BY-SA 4.0)

A flaw in Soviet logistics planning often impeded combat effectiveness in Afghanistan. The common Soviet policy of conserving materiel for larger operations/future use often led to battlefield shortages. As a result, PKM ammunition was delivered in 440-round boxes and then had to be loaded into an ammunition belt by hand or using a hand-cranked loader – thus increasing reloading time in combat. The BMP-2 amphibious infantry fighting vehicle carried two basic loads for the machine gun already belted, but to reload a basic load of 500 rounds of machine-gun ammunition was estimated to take 38 minutes due to the design of the links (Nawroz & Grau 1995: 31).

Soviet doctrine during the war in Afghanistan was that when flanking the Mujahideen in mountainous terrain, deployment and use of the AGS-17 automatic grenade launcher and the PKM were emphasized (Grau & Bartles 2016: 165). Also, once the 5.45×39mm RPK-74 was deployed its limited range made the availability of the 7.62×54mmR PKM or heavier machine guns even more important for longer-range engagement. One result of fighting in Afghanistan, where the closeness of the enemy was not always apparent, was that the Soviets developed a chart of the range at which sound travels at night when the wind is not blowing; according to the chart, loading a machine gun could be heard to 500m (Grau & Bartles 2016: 168).

Soviet doctrine also called for the leader of a Russian squad to prepare his squad's range card to check that there were no gaps or unintentional overlapping fields of fire. The squad machine gun had a primary position in the trench line and also a secondary position to defend against a flanking attack or one from the rear. For night firing or in other situations in which it was hard to observe, stakes might be used to limit the traverse of the machine gun, or the traverse could be set with the tripod. Each machine-gun unit had a "box" into which it fired. An AGS-17 automatic grenade launcher might be used in conjunction with a PKM (Gray & Bartles 2016: 66). In the attack, a motorized rifle squad would be divided into a fire group consisting of the squad leader, grenadier, and machine-gunner, and a maneuver group led by a senior rifleman (Grau & Bartles 2016: 110).

THE IRAN–IRAQ WAR

Mention should be made of the use of Soviet machine guns during the Iran–Iraq War (1980–88). Iran was equipped with the "BB-Kalash" and Iraq with the locally produced "Al Quds," both versions of the RPK. Both armies also fielded versions of the PK, in the case of Iran the PKM/PKT, while Iraq deployed the PKS and PKT, the latter of which was known as the "Be-Ke-Se." Iran also had a version of the DShKM designated the MGD 12.7, while Iraq had a version known as the "Doshka." Reportedly, Iraq received 650 armored personnel carriers, identified as the Model 63 and armed with the DShK, from China.

When considering the use of machine guns in the Iran–Iraq War, some comparisons can be made with World War I as both conflicts involved trench warfare. The Iraqis developed a more sophisticated trench system that was triangular in shape, with a triangle at each corner. A company-sized unit held each of the corner triangles, with machine guns deployed to grant a field of fire covering all directions and even allowing the battalion to keep fighting if outflanked. As the Iranians become more adept on the attack, the Iraqis built a defense in depth with multiples of the triangular trench systems.

At least early in the war, large numbers of Iranian troops martyred themselves in suicidal attacks through minefields in front of Iraqi trench lines amid the machine-gun fire. These "human wave" attacks by Iranians seeking martyrdom were reportedly unsettling, to say the least, to Iraqi troops but as did US troops facing similar Chinese attacks during the Korean War, Iraqis responded with the effective use of tanks, artillery, mines, and machine guns. Owing to the ability of the Iranians to draw troops from a population three times that of Iraq, early in the war the Iraqis tried to rely on tanks without infantry support to crush Iranian infantry. At times, this tactic was disastrous; in some cases because of limitations in the use of the tank-mounted machine guns at close quarters (Pelletiere & Johnson 1991: 59).

The DShKM has been widely used across Africa since the 1960s, arming both national armed forces and insurgents. Here, a Malawi Defence Force soldier fires a DShKM with tank-style grip and non-standard flash hider during a training operation, May 2018. (RP Images/Alamy Stock Photo)

THE CHECHEN WARS

In 1989 the Soviet armed forces left Afghanistan, but five years later in 1994 what is generally known as the "First Chechen War" (1994–96) began, placing Russian troops once again in combat against Muslim fighters, though many Chechens had received military training either in the Soviet Army or in Middle Eastern guerilla warfare training camps.

Building on any training they may have received, the Chechens showed creativity in tailoring the combat elements available to the insurgency war. For example, a Chechen squad might be composed of two men with RPG-7 or RPG-18 rocket launchers, two with machine guns, and often one with a sniping rifle. Such a squad carried a lot of firepower for a hit-and-run engagement or an ambush in an urban area. As can be seen, the Chechens did not use standard military squads. Three such "squads" as mentioned above and a small support group made up a 25-man unit. The support group usually included at least one medic, three ammunition/supply carriers, and two snipers armed with SVD rifles. Note the importance placed on having spare ammunition available for the RPGs and machine guns (Oliker 2001: 45).

When Russian troops entered an ambush's kill zone, Chechen fighters would deploy snipers and machine-gunners to eliminate supporting infantry, while RPG-armed fighters would eliminate the armored vehicles. As the Chechens were well acquainted with Russian equipment, they concentrated their fire on the armored vehicles' fuel cells and engines. These tactics worked so well that an average of only 3–6 hits were needed to knock out each vehicle (Oliker 2001: 46). As had the Mujahideen in Afghanistan, the Chechens learned to take advantage of the elevation limitations of Russian tanks' main guns. To counter the Chechen ambush teams taking advantage of these limitations in main-gun elevation and depression, self-propelled antiaircraft machine-gun-armed vehicles such as the ZSU-23-4 *Shilka* were deployed to eliminate these Chechen assault teams (Oliker 2001: 50).

A Russian soldier armed with a PKM guards a checkpoint in Grozny, April 1995. (Shakh Aivasov/Alamy Stock Photo)

USING THE RPK/RPK-74

The RPK in its various iterations has served as the Soviet and then Russian squad automatic weapon for over 60 years and despite some flaws has performed well. As it is chambered for the standard service rifle cartridge – first the 7.62×39mm and later the 5.45×39mm – logistics are simplified. Its ability to take the longer 40-round (7.62×39mm) or 45-round (5.45×39mm) magazines as well as standard magazines allows the gunner to keep engaging even when his basic load of eight magazines has been emptied. The author has found that the longer magazines may require some care when assuming a prone firing posture, though the bipod normally positions the weapon high enough that the magazines will not drag.

The "club foot" buttstock of the RPK is well shaped to fit snugly against the shoulder and to allow the support hand to press the buttstock tightly and comfortably. The RPK/RPK-74 is light enough that it can be fired offhand while moving between firing positions or advancing, though the gunner must have some arm strength to fire effectively. In the author's experience, a range of about 50m is the maximum for effective offhand firing of short bursts. An experienced gunner might do better. For parachuting or air assault, the folding stock is a real boon, though to engage effectively past point-blank range, deploying the stock is necessary. As there is a semiautomatic setting in standard AK fashion, single-shot "sniping" at longer ranges is possible. Firing from a closed bolt, the RPK/RPK-74 is more likely to overheat, but the necessity to change magazines frequently allows a bit of time for cooling. As the RPK is a squad automatic weapon, continuous area fire is not its primary mission in any case. It should be noted that a 75-round drum magazine is available for the RPK for use when it is emplaced in a defensive position. The author prefers the box magazines, however, because they are easier to carry and rattle less.

Another advantage of the RPK/RPK-74 is its controls are the same as those of an AK-47/AK-74. As a result, should an RPK/RPK-74 gunner become a casualty, a rifleman can easily operate the weapon. On the other hand, the author has found that with RPKs that have seen a lot of use, sometimes the selector becomes loose and has a tendency to drop to the "semiautomatic" position. A fix that the author has used is to use his trigger finger to hold the selector in the full-automatic position while operating the trigger with his middle finger. This would suffice until an armorer could repair the problem.

While firing the RPK from the shoulder the author is actually pulling the trigger with his middle finger and using his trigger finger to keep the selector on "full-auto." This unconventional hold of the weapon can arise if the selector becomes loose. (Author)

The NATO equivalent of the RPK/RPK-74 is the FN Minimi/M249, which is heavier, but also allows more sustained fire. The M249 Para model weighs only 7.3kg and is just 893mm in overall length. For comparison, the RPK weighs 4.8kg and is 1,040mm in overall length. Though designed to be belt fed, the M249 can also take a STANAG (NATO standard) magazine if desired so it shares the ability to use an infantryman's rifle magazine if necessary. Either weapon offers a base of fire for an infantry squad. The RPK/RPK-74 may be more suited to Russian tactics, especially currently with conscript infantrymen, as it will require less training.

It is interesting to note the overview to the RPK given in the *US Army Special Forces Foreign Weapons Handbook*, as the summary is designed for troops who will face the RPK and those who may well train indigenous personnel in its use:

The Soviet 7.62-mm Ruchnoi Pulemet Kalashnikov (RPK) is the standard Soviet Squad Light Machinegun. It has replaced the RPD Light Machinegun. The RPK is identical to the AK Assault Rifle as far as operation and major component parts are concerned. It is essentially an AK with a longer barrel, modified stock and a bipod attached. It is an extremely well made weapon. It is fed from a curved 40 round capacity box magazine or a 100 round capacity drum magazine. The barrel is chrome lined as are those of the standard AK series of weapons. It is chambered for the Soviet M1943 intermediate cartridge as are the other two standard Soviet Squad weapons, the SKS Carbine and the AK Assault Rifle. The Soviet Infantry Squad, due to the elimination of the RPD, now has only one automatic weapon system to learn and maintain, the AK and the RPK. (US Army 1967: 324)

As special-forces troops will often encounter foreign weapons in use with indigenous troops whom they will train, the most prescient point in the summary is the advantage of having just one system for training personnel.

The author firing the RPK-74 with bipod extended and a 45-round magazine in place; note that positioning the bipod near the crest of the hill allows firing from cover. (Author)

During the First Chechen War, many of the weapons used by the insurgents had been seized from Russian armories, with the RPK and PK/PKM providing the Chechens' LMGs and MMGs. A standard Chechen tactic was illustrated on June 14, 1995, when Chechen fighters seized buildings in the town of Budyonnovsk on the border with Russia. Machine guns were emplaced on the rooftops of buildings, hostages were taken, and buildings including the local hospital were booby-trapped. During the assault by Russian *spetsnaz* on June 17, snipers eliminated some Chechen snipers and machine-gun crews, but not all of them. As a result, not all of the hostages were released at the conclusion of the crisis on June 19 and the Chechens were allowed to return to Chechnya.

In August 1999, after a three-year hiatus, fighting between Russian and Chechen forces resumed in what became the Second Chechen War (1999–2009). During the Russian assault on Grozny, the capital city of Chechnya, which lasted from December 25, 1999, to February 6, 2000, the fighting for Minutka Square was especially bloody. Both sides fought to gain the "high ground" in the form of multistory buildings surrounding the square. To clear these buildings, the Russians utilized a unit split into three tactical groups: an assault group made up of fast-moving, mobile soldiers armed with light automatic weapons (AK-74 and AKS-74); a cover group to provide covering fire, armed with RPG-7s and machine guns (RPK-74 and PK/PKM); and a support group with mortars and a reserve supply of ammunition for the weapons used by all three groups (Oliker 2001: 68). Eventually, it took mortar fire and a covering smoke screen for the Russian assault troops to secure the rooftops.

A Russian door gunner, most likely from the MVD, on a reconnaissance flight over Chechnya in April 1995, mans what appears to be the PKB version of the PK, which is fitted with double "spade" grips and door mounts. Note also the "antiaircraft" front sight. (Chris Booth/Alamy Stock Photo)

Two Chechen fighters, one with a PKM, head toward the front line in Pervomaiskoye, Chechnya, December 1994. The Chechen at left may look warlike with his machine gun enveloped in its ammunition belt, but untangling the belt would take undue time and delay bringing the weapon into action – and the long belt would likely get entangled or become kinked. (Alexander Zemlianichenko/Alamy Stock Photo)

The 12.7×108mm Kord, which entered service in 2001, offered a useful "light heavy machine gun," which with a bipod weighed just 31kg; light enough to carry onto rooftops during urban combat, though it takes a strong gunner to carry it alone. Contributing to its effectiveness, recoil is surprisingly light, even with the bipod.

Reportedly, Chechen fighters were trained on a vast array of weapons so that whatever they captured they could use. Based on captured Chechen written material, an attack on a Russian position would be carried out by a group divided into three. RPGs and PKs were placed in support positions at least 50m from the target (Oliker 2001: 94). Another Chechen tactic was to hide in reinforced basements (in effect bunkers) from which two- or three-man teams armed with RPGs and PKs would emerge to attack Russian forces with massed fire. After a quick engagement, the Chechens would retreat into the basements. Some of these basement bunkers even had an additional well dug beneath them to give the Chechens even more protection. Eventually, the Russians used a team of two tanks and a ZSU-23-4 *Shilka* to destroy the bunkers (Oliker 2001: 78).

In their iteration of the "Technical" so widely used in Afghanistan, Somalia, and elsewhere, the Chechens mounted mortars, antiaircraft guns, automatic grenade launchers, KPVTs and DShKMs in the backs of trucks (Oliker 2001: 94). It should be noted that the Chechens realized the value of the PK and RPK in their hit-and-run tactics and, hence, appreciated the importance of well-trained, experienced machine-gunners (Thomas 2007: 764).

Russian machine guns have also proliferated in Central and South America. Here, in a 2013 photograph, a Peruvian soldier keeps watch with his PKM, mounted aboard a Russian-supplied Mi-17 helicopter. (Galeria del Ministerio de Defensa del Perú/Wikimedia/CC BY 2.0)

NORTHERN IRELAND

The Irish Republican Army also made use of the DShKM against British forces during "The Troubles" (1968–98). In January 1999, three DShKMs were found in a cache in County Monaghan in the Irish Republic near the border with Northern Ireland (Cleary & Cusack 2011). Reportedly, 18 DShKMs were acquired by the IRA from Libya and were used to shoot down a British Army Air Corps (AAC) Lynx helicopter in County Armagh on June 23, 1988. The DShKM was also employed during an unsuccessful ambush of a Royal Air Force Puma helicopter and four AAC Lynxes in County Armagh on September 23, 1993. The Puma and one of the Lynxes were hit during the action. (Roblin 2021).

AFGHANISTAN 2001–21

Post 9/11, US forces faced Russian machine guns in the hands of the Taliban. US troops acting as advisors and trainers of the Afghan National Army also had to be proficient in the use of various Russian weapons. Among the weapons left over from the Soviet–Afghan War and in the hands of the Taliban were the DShK, KPV, PK, RPD, RPK, and SG-43. In fact, some of the first US Special Forces troops to enter Afghanistan, a small number of horse-borne troops operating with members of the Northern Alliance, found that the Afghans were employing 19th-century tactics against PKs (Stanton 2009: 172).

US troops continued to assist Afghan National Army troops long after the initial incursion to drive Al-Qaeda from Afghanistan. In response, the

Taliban became more sophisticated in their tactics and use of machine guns. For example, during an ambush in Farah Province in 2007, Taliban fighters fired machine guns from a group of typical Afghan fortified compounds to outflank a large US/Afghan patrol. The Taliban also became skilled at using fire-and-movement and setting ambushes (Meyerle & Malkasian 2009: 5).

Using tactics originally developed by the Mujahideen, the Taliban ambushed Coalition helicopters from standoff positions on the heights overlooking an LZ using RPGs and HMGs (Meyerle & Malkasian 2009: 7). During 2007 and 2008, the Taliban's relatively small assault groups approached British bases stealthily and attacked them in Helmand Province, again using RPGs and HMGs (Meyerle & Malkasian 2009: 8). Coalition convoys also came under HMG fire. MMGs, as well as AK-74s and RPGs, were used by attackers from prepared positions at ranges up to 100m. In many of the ambushes faced by US Marine Corps convoys, the combination of PKs and RPGs was used at ranges of 75m and less (Meyerle & Malkasian 2009: 38).

There seemed to be no shortage of PKs, as the Taliban would often use substantial numbers in attacks on firebases. For example, on June 5, 2006, insurgents firing recoilless rifles, PKs, AK-47s, and mortars attacked Firebase Chalekor from eight directions. They were eventually driven off, but it took fire from the defenders' 60mm mortars, 105mm artillery pieces using direct fire, and air strikes (Meyerle & Malkasian 2009: 54). In the June 2008 assault on Sarpoza Prison in Kandahar City, during which around 1,000 prisoners were freed, the Taliban made use of one of their

An Afghan National Army soldier cradles his RPK with drum magazine during Operation *Charkh Restoration*, April 2011. Although the RPK is not immediately ready to fire when carried in this fashion, this is a far better way to handle the weight of the weapon and a full 75-round magazine than leaning the weapon against the wall. (Sergeant Sean Casey/Wikimedia/Public Domain)

The KPV in antiaircraft use: cooling a recently fired ZPU-1 in Khowst Province, Afghanistan, September 2009. (Matthew Freire, US Army/Wikimedia/Public Domain)

"belt fed machine guns" to shoot the locks off the prison doors (Meyerle & Malkasian 2009: 70).

In May 2005, a 15-man squad of the Afghan National Police along with eight members of the British Army's Parachute Regiment encountered a group of Taliban commanders guarded by more than 70 well-armed insurgents. The insurgents attacked with PKM GPMGs and RPK LMGs as well as RPGs and based on their volume of fire had plenty of ammunition. Eventually, Parachute Regiment machine-gunners were landed by helicopter and helped the Coalition troops to gain fire superiority (Meyerle & Malkasian 2009: 84).

In 2006, ambushes were initiated by Taliban guerrillas using RPKs and RPGs, a combination that lent itself well to hit-and-run usage. Insurgents also developed ambush tactics against Coalition armored vehicles. PK gunners would open fire on the turret gunners of the vehicles, while firing volleys of RPG rounds from the front to disable the vehicle. The intent was to set the vehicle on fire, then target US Marines or other troops with machine-gun fire as they exited the vehicle (Meyerle & Malkasian 2009: 114).

Michael Golembesky, a US Marine Corps veteran who served in Afghanistan in 2010, elucidates how effective the DShKM was in the hands of the Taliban. With one DShK, Taliban fighters overlooking the Marines' position could threaten C-130 Hercules transport aircraft or helicopters arriving at their Forward Operating Base (Golembesky 2016: 35–36). He also notes that the Taliban often used their DShKMs without the tripod, which had been scavenged to repair a vehicle or something else. Instead, they hung ropes from trees and affixed them to the weapon. Reportedly, recoil was excessive, but they could still fire short bursts.

IRAQ 2003–11

Following the invasion of Iraq on March 20, 2003, Coalition forces encountered such large quantities of Russian machine guns – PK/PKMs, RPKs, DShKMs, etc. – that US troops received training in their use and maintenance. This was especially true of the US Marines, who trained Iraqi military and law-enforcement personnel in the maintenance and use of Russian weapons, especially the PKM. Iraqi forces were given US weapons such as the M240 and M249, but the PK/PKM and DShKM remained in use. The Marines also trained some Iraqi troops in use of the RPK.

Many of the weapons in Iraqi arsenals dated from the 1970s and had been provided primarily by the old ComBloc countries. For example, US Marines captured a large number of Russian PKMs in Iraq. Iraqi police subsequently used the Bulgarian MG-1M, which accounts for the large number of photographs showing Iraqi security forces with fluted-barrel PKMs. Some North Korean PK derivatives such as the Type 73 and Type 82 also turned up in Iraq. Even some of the US M1A1 main battle tanks supplied to Iraq later had their machine guns changed to Russian 12.7×108mm weapons.

For their part, Iraqi insurgents used an array of weapons including versions of the RPK designated the RBK, Al-Quds, Al-Kuds, or Al-Guds,

An Iraqi special-operations forces soldier poses with what appears to be a PK, but with an unusually long barrel, August 2004. The longer barrel and the flash suppressor appear to be those of the PKT, which would normally be mounted on a tank. (Gunnery Sergeant Chago Zapata, USMC/Wikimedia/Public Domain)

A US advisor coaches an Iraqi soldier in firing a PK variant. (DVIDS/Public Domain)

and versions of the PK/PKM such as the PKS, PKC, or BKC (US Army 2004). Rugged and easy to maintain, these ComBloc weapons were popular among Iraqi insurgents, one reason being the ready and cheaper availability of inexpensive 7.62×54mmR and 12.7×108mm ammunition. Multiple weapons caches captured in Iraq contained hundreds of Russian-derived machine guns. The DShKM and KPV were widely used on trucks (i.e. the Iraqi version of the "Technical"), which posed a threat to Coalition helicopters. At least some API ammunition was captured from insurgents.

US contractors often used ComBloc machine guns, especially the RPK and PK/PKM. These weapons could be purchased locally or on the surplus weapons market and allowed security companies to arm their personnel less expensively. Some of the companies supplying contractors hired enough special-operations troops who had been trained on ComBloc weapons that they could train team members who had not been. Often, the ComBloc weapons acquired on the world market needed to be refurbished; hence, some contract gunsmiths with knowledge of these weapons were hired.

As well as US weapons, these contractors made extensive use of the RPK and PK/PKM in the hands of a "tail gunner" bringing up the rear of a motorcade, this individual being responsible for monitoring traffic approaching from the rear and engaging threats. In situations where contractor operations were subsequently investigated, the use of locally sourced weapons and ammunition made it harder for the investigators to attribute controversial actions to the contractors.

A Kurdish Peshmerga (special forces) officer in training, Mosul, Iraq, May 2007. He is firing the PKM offhand, grasping the barrel-change handle with his support hand. (Staff Sergeant Vanessa Valentine, USAF/Wikimedia/Public Domain)

During training in 2007, an Iraqi soldier fires a PK-derived variant while his assistant gunner holds the belt to keep it feeding reliably. (USMC/Public Domain)

This still from an ISIS propaganda video shows an Islamic State fighter near Manjib, Syria, in July 2016. He can take advantage of firing from the prone position with his PK-type machine gun. Many insurgent fighters do not use a box for their ammunition belt, which in dusty conditions can affect reliable feeding. (Handout/Alamy Stock Photo)

THE SYRIAN CIVIL WAR

From March 2011, the conflict in Syria and nearby countries involved the use of large quantities of former ComBloc weapons alongside those from around the world. Weapons up to a century old have been encountered, along with some creative "modernizations" of weapons that might be viewed as obsolete. The inventory of the Syrian Arab Army at the beginning of the conflict included Soviet, Russian, Chinese, and North Korean machine guns, these being joined by many other types as the insurgency spread. Chinese weapons reportedly entered Syria via Sudan, while other weapons used by the Syrian opposition seem to have come from Croatian stockpiles, as well as ammunition from Croatian-controlled stockpiles of former Yugoslav weapons.

Insurgents made extensive use of HMGs during the Syrian Civil War (2011–24), notably the Chinese W85 HMG, a "product-improved" DShKM offering the advantage that insurgents already trained on the DShKM could easily learn to operate the W85. Used primarily against the

Airbase incursion, Syria, c.2016 (opposite)

A detachment of Russian military police manning a checkpoint at an airbase in Syria is using TIGR infantry mobility vehicles. The TIGR at left mounts a Kord HMG with 6C21 remote-control firing capability primarily in the counterdrone mission. The gunner in the TIGR at right mans a Kord 6P49 ready to engage against an attempt to infiltrate the airbase. The soldier on foot is armed with an AK-74M assault rifle. The wall in the foreground has been breached by a previous rocket attack and shields an ISIS infiltrator armed with a Pecheneg GPMG, which was designed to be more accurate than the PKM GPMG. As the Pecheneg was often in use with *spetsnaz* units, this example was possibly captured or stolen from an armory.

A Kurdish militiaman balances his PK variant on a wall in Rojava, Syria, January 2017. (Chris Huby/Le Pictorium/Alamy Stock Photo)

Assad regime's aircraft, some W85s have been equipped with an antiaircraft optical sight. According to one source, the W85 was actually more common than the real DShKM. Anti-ISIS Syrian insurgents made considerable use of PKM variants, including some mounted on improvised armored vehicles, often based on a bulldozer. Vehicles of this kind would be armored with steel plates and armed with machine guns mounted in turrets, but proved to be easily disabled by RPGs. Another vehicle, based on the Toyota Hilux 4×4 pickup, proved more useful. These "armored cars" mounted a 12.7mm or 14.5mm HMG in an improvised armored turret.

ISIS often demonstrated deadly creativity in its use of improvised tactics and weapons, often shifting between conventional warfare, guerrilla warfare, and terrorism. For example, in order to preserve ISIS manpower, sniper rifles and machine guns were reportedly modified to fire remotely using video-game controllers and television screens. Anti-ISIS Syrian insurgents mounted DShKMs on motorcycles, while others fielded PKMs shortened to "bullpup" configuration. Captured Assad regime armor provided another source of machine guns. For example, the Soviet-made MT-LB tracked armored personnel carrier mounted an NSV or Kord HMG and the Tigr-M 4×4 armored personnel carrier mounted a Pecheneg GPMG and a Kord.

UKRAINE

Russia's full-scale invasion of Ukraine in 2022 sparked a conflict in which every Russian machine-gun type in use since 1900 would play at least some role, as Ukraine stripped military museums of weapons including PM M1910s. As the PM M1910 chambers the same 7.62×54mmR cartridge as the PK/PKM, logistics is not a problem. Left over from Ukraine's days as part of the Soviet Union, Cold War-era machine guns remain in use with Ukrainian troops as well as Russian forces, which have reportedly used World War I and World War II machine guns as well.

One machine gun inherited from the Soviet armed forces and put to use by the Ukrainians is the DShK/DShKM. When the Soviet Union collapsed in 1991, the Ukrainian Army inherited thousands of vehicle-mounted DShKMs. Many of these have been removed from the vehicles and modified to serve as infantry-support weapons. Initially developed in 2014 for fighting against Russian forces in the Donbas region, these modifications include the fitting of a larger muzzle brake as well as a pistol grip and shoulder stock. A bipod to allow firing from the prone position was also added. Crewed by a two-person team, these modified weapons have proven effective in trench warfare. When such weapons are fitted with a scope, a gunner and observer can engage targets with precision out to 500m (Newton 2022).

As their supply of missiles to knock down Russian drones has become depleted, the Ukrainians have deployed HMGs, which receive information from sensors that help calculate target data on the drones. This system consists of "heavy machine guns, with thermal scopes and tablets paired on a gun mount." Various types of sensor (i.e. radar, acoustics, etc.) are deployed around Ukrainian cities and the data fed to the machine-gunners. Another makeshift "sensor system" consists of thousands of cell phones paired with microphones mounted on 1.8m poles. As an example of the

Pictured at a Russian-backed rebel position in eastern Ukraine in June 2015, this tripod-mounted PKM has an improvised buttstock repair. (Mstyslav Chernov/Wikimedia/CC BY-SA 4.0)

New York State National Guardsmen learning to fire the DShKM while training with Ukrainian troops. (DVIDS/Public Domain)

successful use of this "low tech" system, 80 out of 84 Russian drones were knocked down in one day's engagements (Gosselin-Malo 2024).

In another creative use of technology, the Ukrainians have developed ground drones mounting HMGs. Reportedly, Russia is also developing its own unmanned ground vehicles. Ukrainian strike units have also used their own version of a "Technical," a pickup truck with a mounted 12.7×108mm NSV *Utyos* along with a 60mm mortar and its crew. The truck would bring the NSV to bear from 1.5km while the mortar crew would dismount at that distance and launch mortar bombs while the NSV's gunner fired up to 50 rounds. Afterwards the truck would move to a new firing point (Anonymous 2022a).

As Russia finds itself in a war of attrition, its troops are facing an array of Soviet and Russian machine guns in the hands of Ukrainian troops. Both the Russians and the Ukrainians know the strengths and shortcomings of the weapons they face, as well as how to refurbish captured weapons and immediately turn them against the enemy. The 7.62×54mmR cartridge, in service since 1891, is still used by both sides. It could be posited that the most influential aspect of Russian machine guns in use today is the longevity of this venerable cartridge.

Russian weapons upgrades and tactical innovations using machine guns have also occurred. At least partially to address Russia's shortage of manpower as losses have increased, the Russian Army, based on lessons learned from the Wagner Group, have begun using assault companies, which conserve manpower while maximizing firepower.

SHOOTING THE PK/PKM

With the PK, the Soviet Army finally had a GPMG chambered for a substantial cartridge: the long-serving 7.62×54mmR. Though the PK's feed system necessitates use of a "claw" to pull cartridges from the belt, then deposit them on the feed tray, in the author's experience the weapon is very reliable. Its open-bolt design helps avoid overheating and allows efficient cooling as air can flow through the barrel and ejection port. A quick-change barrel also aids sustained fire when the PK/PKM is used on the defense. The author has found that the barrel lock, located beneath the feed tray, which must be used to allow a barrel change is easily located and operated with practice.

The sights for the PK/PKM are somewhat optimistic as they are of AK-47 type with increments between 100m and 1,500m. The fact they are similar to AK-47 sights makes training gunners a bit easier, however. Far better are the versions of the PK/PKM with a siderail and optical sights. The standard optic encountered by the author has been the 4×26mm 1P29. A feature the author has found particularly useful on the PK/PKM is the wooden skeleton stock, which is of particular use when firing from the prone position as the support hand can grasp the stock and push it against the shoulder, thus keeping it in place when firing bursts. Another feature of the PKM that helps when firing longer and more continuous bursts is the three-position gas regulator.

Preparing to fire the PKM is a similar process as used for most belt-fed machine guns. First, the cocking handle it pulled to the rear to cock the bolt; then it is run forward. Next, the feed tray is lifted to check the chamber is empty. Then, the trigger is pulled to run the bolt forward. With the bolt forward, the ammunition belt is pulled across the feed tray right to left, taking care the rim of the cartridge fits into the "claw" horns. The top cover is then closed and locked. At this point, the cocking handle is pulled to the rear to cock the bolt; then the handle is run forward again. The PKM is then ready to fire or if combat is not imminent, the safety may be applied.

Although the PKM is intended to be fired by a gunner who is either seated with the tripod or prone with the bipod, if necessary while moving with the weapon, a short burst can be fired from the hip. As there is not a forearm, the author has found that it is necessary to grasp the base of the box containing the ammunition belt or grip the bipod, the latter option being the more desirable as the weight of the weapon is spread out. After one short burst, the PKM's barrel has risen off the target. For all practical purposes, shooting offhand is futile, though at close range it might cause an attacker to duck for cover!

The author firing the PKM from the Stepanov tripod while seated; note that the PKM's stock may be grasped by the support hand for better control. (Author)

Ukrainian and Oklahoma National Guard troops firing the DShKM during joint training; the flash offers a good view of the effect of the DShKM's horizontal muzzle brake. (DVIDS/Public Domain)

An assault company is normally composed of two 12–15-strong assault platoons plus three fire-support platoons, with the following armament: four BMP or BMD-2 infantry fighting vehicles; one T-72 main battle tank; two AGS-17 automatic grenade launchers; two Kord HMGs; two antitank guided missiles; two sniper pairs; two 82mm or 120mm mortars; and one 122mm D30 howitzer or 120mm 2S9 self-propelled mortar (Roblin 2023).

There is also a report that as of June 2023, the Kord is being upgraded to increase its capability of firing a continuous burst without the need for a barrel change from 100 to 300 rounds. The upgraded weapons are installed on remotely controlled modules for armored vehicles or helicopters. Among the solutions being considered for overheating are a barrel alloy maintaining its functionality over a wider range of temperatures or using a ribbed barrel to aid in heat transfer through greater air exposure (Anonymous 2023).

Ukraine has also repurposed many of the PKTs salvaged from destroyed Russian tanks and converted them for ground use by fabricating a stock and pistol-grip assembly. The stock developed by Ukrainian technicians slides into the PKT's trunnion where the solenoid was formerly located. Once the stock is fitted, the pistol grip (reportedly an AK-47 type) and trigger assembly is pivoted up and secured by a cross pin. The sear located inside the PKT is triggered by a hook projecting from the trigger mechanism. It should be noted that Ukrainian armorers most likely knew of adaptions of PKTs during the Chechen Wars. It also appears that Russia's Tula Arsenal has developed its own kit for converting the PKT for infantry usage (Anonymous 2022b).

IMPACT
Global influence

An indication of the widespread use of the RPD by insurgents around the world can be gleaned from its involvement in more than 40 conflicts ranging from the Vietnam War, Yom Kippur War, Soviet–Afghan War, Iran–Iraq War, Gulf War, Syrian Civil War, and current Russia–Ukraine War to lesser-known conflicts such as the Ivorian civil wars (2002–07 and 2010–11) and the OLA Insurgency (2018–) and Tigray War (2020–22) in Ethiopia. In many cases, RPDs that have served in earlier conflicts have been acquired by arms dealers or intelligence agencies to equip forces in a more recent war. Other Soviet and Russian machine guns have been similarly widely used across the globe. Not only are the RPD and RPK highly effective weapons for use in ambushes set by insurgents, but they have also served as status symbols, especially in insurgencies in Africa and the Islamic world.

The RPK-74M, pictured in the hands of Russia's MVD (*Ministerstvo vnutrennikh del*, Ministry of Internal Affairs), 2010. MVD troops are well trained, as shown by this man's stable firing position, the confident way he has the RPK pulled tight against his shoulder, and cheek weld. (Vitaly V. Kuzmin/Wikimedia/CC BY-SA 4.0)

US Marines practice-firing Kalashnikov-designed small arms, among them an RPK (at left), September 1989. (Unknown/Wikimedia/Public Domain)

LOGISTICAL ADVANTAGES

A crucial influence of the post-1945 Soviet/Russian machine guns was the chambering of the RPD and RPK for the intermediate 7.62×39mm cartridge. Not only did this ease the logistics of ammunition supply, but it also allowed development of a lighter squad automatic weapon for ease of transport during the advance. To highlight how forward-thinking this was, consider the fact that the RPD entered service in the 1940s, while the FN Minimi, the NATO squad automatic weapon chambered for the intermediate 5.56×45mm round, did not enter service until the late 1970s.

Instead, the United States and other NATO countries developed an "intermediate, intermediate" cartridge in the 7.62×51mm NATO cartridge designed for "battle rifles" such as the M14, G3, and FN FAL. LMGs developed for the 7.62×51mm round such as the US M60, Belgian FN MAG, and German MG3, were still MMGs, though the M60 was somewhat more portable and served US forces for decades as a squad automatic weapon. The M60, entering service in 1957, lost any logistical advantages of a machine gun chambering the same round as the service rifle upon adoption of the 5.56×45mm-caliber M16 in 1964. It was not until 1982 that the United States adopted the 5.56×45mm M249 version of the FN Minimi as a squad automatic weapon. Admittedly, the M249 is a more effective squad automatic weapon than the RPD, but it was also decades later on the scene.

The RPK and the later RPK-74 are definitely not as effective in the squad automatic role as the FN Minimi or the RPD, but they are portable

An emplaced DShKM in Syrian Arab Army hands, Damascus, March 2018. (Xinhua/Alamy Stock Photo)

US Marines in training with Finnish troops in 2022 firing the 12.7mm NSV. One of the more interesting aspects of Russian machine guns during the 21st century is the familiarity with them now common among US troops who have faced them in Afghanistan, Iraq, Syria, and elsewhere and who have also had the mission of training "proxy" troops in these same venues in uses of the RPD, PKM, and other Russian machine guns. (DVIDS/Public Domain)

and may be fired while advancing. They also take not only the same cartridge as the Russian service rifle but the same magazines, though larger-capacity feed devices are available. Another advantage of the RPK/RPK-74 as a squad automatic weapon is that its operation is the same as the standard Russian AK service rifle; thus should the gunner become a casualty any member of the squad can operate it.

It may also be argued that the RPD and RPK had a significant influence on Soviet-backed insurgencies. These weapons were chambered for the same 7.62×39mm cartridge as the SKS battle rifles and AK-47 assault rifles with which insurgents were armed, thus easing their tenuous supply situation. The RPD and especially the RPK lent themselves to use by poorly trained guerrilla forces. The weapons were designed to keep operating in adverse conditions and were well-suited to being carried by smaller-statured insurgents in Asia.

Also used by numerous armies within the former Soviet sphere of influence and insurgents that received Soviet aid, the RPK has proven popular because of chambering the ubiquitous 7.62×39mm cartridge and also because it may be easily carried by the individual fighter. The RPK has also seen wide usage with various resistance groups as well as armies within the Soviet/Russian sphere of influence. As with the RPD, the ability of the RPK to fire standard 7.62×39mm cartridges has made it an effective weapon even in small cells of fighters. As it will also function with standard AK-47 magazines as well as the extended magazines designed for it, the RPK requires little in the way of logistic support.

THE PKM VS THE FN MAG

The PKM and FN MAG are beyond doubt the world's two most widely used GPMGs at the time of writing. To some extent each is illustrative of its origins with the former Warsaw Pact and NATO. Millions of these weapons have been manufactured and both have seen extensive use in combat. Having fired quite a few rounds through both GPMGs, the author will offer his views on the two weapons.

From the point of view of a gunner who will carry the machine gun into combat and deploy it, weight is an important issue. At 9kg, the PKM has a marked advantage over the MAG at 11.8kg. The US M240B version of the MAG is even heavier, at 12.5kg. The M122A1 tripod for the M240 adds 10.99kg. The PKMS with the Stepanov-designed tripod weighs just over 12kg. In standard configuration, the MAG has a slightly greater overall length at 1,263mm versus 1,203mm for the PKM. A shorter and lighter version of the MAG, designated the MAG 10.10, is available.

There is little difference in practical performance between the 7.62×54mmR cartridge for which the PKM is chambered and the 7.62×51mm NATO cartridge for which the MAG/M240B is chambered.

Both weapons fire from an open bolt and fire on full-automatic only. Both allow quick change of a barrel, though the MAG/M240B barrel change is a bit smoother. For carrying, the M240B's barrel-changing handle may be moved to the center. Many gunners, though, choose to use a two-point sling for carrying. A barrel change with the PKM is slowed due to the need to push a wedge out before removing the barrel. Note that only the front sights located on the barrels are adjustable for windage on both the MAG/M240B and PKM.

An advantage of the MAG/M240B in continuous firing is the use of M13 disintegrating links, which along with spent cartridges fall downwards. The MAG/M240B feeds from the left while the PKM feeds from the right. Some gunners feel that the left feed is better as the support hand can reach out to guide the belt/linked ammunition if needed. Loading from the left normally makes for a quicker reload by an assistant gunner; however, a well-trained assistant on the PKM can mitigate this difference. Right-handed gunners also have to be more aware of hand and arm placement with the PKM. Use of ammunition belts in the PKM results in the spent belt dangling from the left side of the weapon, which can get in the way if the gunner has to move quickly. The belts are durable and have an easy-to-use pull-through tab.

Both the PKM and MAG/M240B are known for their reliability. The PKM has a three-position gas regulator that allows adjustment when the weapon has built up residue from firing continuously, thus enhancing reliability. The regulator is designed so that adjustments can be made with a cartridge case. The MAG/M240B does not have a gas regulator (its setting is around 600rd/min), but it has a reputation for firing thousands of rounds without any malfunctions. One other note on reliability: for those not familiar with the "claw" system used on the PKM, it may look complicated but it has proven very reliable.

TACTICAL INNOVATION

The PK/PKM has also been a standby weapon for many insurgents and Russian/Chinese/Iranian proxies. A true GPMG, it has given its users an effective "base of fire" weapon, which allows for more sophisticated small-unit tactics for units with the training to deploy the weapon properly. At the time of writing, the PKM has seen action with both sides during the Russian invasion of Ukraine, in some cases deployed to sweep "No Man's Land," much as its precursors did during World War I. The PKM has also been the preeminent GPMG with the Wagner Group during its operations in Ukraine and its short-lived "rebellion." Of course, the shortage of PKMs has resulted in both Russian and Ukrainian forces using machine guns from World War II and even earlier. As the PKM uses the same 7.62×54mmR cartridge as the earlier machine guns, the ammunition supply chain is simplified. Palestinians battling the Israeli Defense Forces in Gaza have deployed Iranian-made versions of the RPD and PKM.

An important aspect of Russian machine guns has been the increased training in their use by US troops. Traditionally, special-operations units

The safety of the MAG/M240B is of the push-through type while that of the PKM is of the "switch" type, which must be rotated. Though not a major issue, the push-through type is slightly faster. Both the PKM and the MAG/M240B have bipods, which work effectively, though the author considers the MAG/240B bipod to be sturdier. With both weapons, if the bipod is folded and locked securely in place, it may be grasped with the support hand when firing from the shoulder or hip. Both weapons may be mounted on tripods for area fire. The Russians issue a pistol grip for the PKM that can attach between the bipod and box magazine to allow better control when shooting from the hip while advancing. Balance of the PKM is also better for hip or offhand shooting.

The buttstocks on both weapons are designed to allow placing of the support hand to push the stock against the shoulder, but the author has a preference for the skeleton stock on the PKM, which allows for gripping with the support hand. A hydraulic buffer on the M240B helps reduce felt recoil.

Both weapons have feed port and ejection port covers that snap shut when not feeding or ejecting, thus preventing debris from getting into the action. Being Kalashnikov-based, the PKM is slightly more "soldier proof" than the MAG/M240B as small parts are less likely to become lost when stripping the weapon.

Both weapons have open sights that are adjustable for elevation. The author has found those of the MAG/M240B to be more usable at longer ranges than the PKM sights. Use of tracer ammunition is, of course, useful at longer distances. The MAG/M240B, and later versions of the PKM, all have the capability to mount optical sights, which increases effective long-range firing dramatically. One point that should be noted is that the M240B has an upper hand guard, which can help mitigate heat mirage with optical sights during continuous firing. Also, laser-aiming devices such as the AN/PEQ-15 Advanced Target Pointer Illuminator Aiming Laser help longer-range engagement with the M240B. Although the author is not familiar with a Russian laser-aiming device for the PKM, one likely exists. Mounting on NATO-type Picatinny rails also allows more precise zeroing with the MAG/M240B than on the Russian side mounts that allow the device to be slid on and locked with the PKM.

M240B gunners consider that the top cover of the M240B may be dropped with the bolt either forward or rearward, which is a distinct advantage as it allows quieter loading when close to the enemy. Loading with the top cover closed in combat also protects the optics from fogging or other problems caused by a heated barrel.

Both the PKM and MAG/M240B are fine weapons, attested to by their wide use. Based on the author's own experience and that of contacts with recent combat experience with both weapons, the feeling of many who are in special-operations or line-infantry units is that given their choice they would like the PKM for patrolling, but the M240B when firing from a static defensive position, especially if likely to engage at ranges greater than 600m.

have received foreign weapons training, but US commitments in Afghanistan, Iraq, and other countries using these weapons has resulted in substantial numbers of US Marines and Army infantrymen receiving training in their use and maintenance so they can advise and train local troops to operate them effectively. The US Marine Corps has even published excellent manuals on the RPD and PKM. The United States also acquired large numbers of Russian machine guns to issue to Afghan and Iraqi police or military units. Of course, the unintended consequence has been that many US troops have died as a result of these weapons falling into enemy hands.

The venerable DShK and DShKM continue to serve as well, though in Russian front-line service the DShKM has been mostly replaced by the 12.7×108mm NSV and Kord HMGs. The Ukrainians have, however, repurposed their DShKMs, left over from when they were part of the Soviet Union, to counter Iranian-made drones being used by the Russians. These weapons are mated with searchlights and CCTV cameras.

CLONES AND LICENSED COPIES

If imitation is, indeed the best form of flattery, the countries that have produced their own versions of the machine guns discussed in this book have flattered Russian designers.

As with many other Soviet weapons, former allies of the Soviet Union also produced copies of the DShK. These included China, which produced a variant of the DShKM designated the Type 54; Albania, which produced a version of the Type 54; Czechoslovakia, which produced the TK Vz.53, one version of which had four barrels; Iran, which produced the DShKM variant designated the MGD 12.7; Pakistan, with a variant of the Type 54; Romania, with the RomArm SA, a locally produced armored-vehicle version; and Ukraine, which produces its own version (Jones 2007: 382).

The RPD has seen use in virtually every conflict since World War II, though major users such as Russia and China replaced it decades ago. Still, the RPD was produced in countries other than the Soviet Union. Most notably, these include China, which produced the Type 56 and 56-1 at Norinco; Egypt, which produced the Type 7.62 Suez at Maadi; and North Korea, which produced the Type 62 at North Korean State Factories

German Democratic Republic (East Germany) border troops, one armed with an RPK clone, presumably an indigenously produced LMGK, in November 1978. The LMGK gave the country's border guards a "longer reach" to engage individuals attempting to escape across the border. (dpa picture alliance/Alamy Stock Photo)

A Hungarian Army soldier armed with a PKM, pictured during training exercises in North Carolina, USA, in August 1996. (NB/ROD/Alamy Stock Photo)

(Jones 2007: 388). Seventy or more countries have used or continue to use the RPD, including the United States, which modified captured RPDs for use by MACV-SOG operators during the Vietnam War. DS Arms in the United States has also produced a semiautomatic version of the RPD.

The RPK has also been produced in various countries, including: Albania, as the Ash-78 Tip-2; Bulgaria, produced by Bulgaria's Arsenal as the LMG-F and available in three calibers (7.62×39mm, 5.45×39mm, and 5.56×45mm NATO); Iraq, as the Al Quds; Romania, produced by Fabrica

A Yugoslavian M72B1, based on the RPK and manufactured by Zastava Arms. Note the distinctive buttstock shape and the fluted barrel to aid cooling. The Iraqi Al Quds variant is based on this design. (Military Images/Alamy Stock Photo)

de Arme Cugir SA as the Pusca Mitralieră md. 1964 (7.62×39mm) and md. 1993 (5.45×39mm); and Serbia, by Zastava Arms as the M72. Formerly, it was produced by East Germany as the LMGK (Jones 2007: 389).

The PK/PKM became the standard GPMG among ComBloc forces as well as Soviet/Russian client states. It was also produced by various countries in various guises. China produced the Type 80 copy of the PKM/PKMS, but also has offered a 7.62×51mm NATO version designated the CS/LM4. Other counties, formerly members of the Warsaw Pact but now members of NATO, have produced copies of the PKM. Poland's Cegielski-Poznań SA experimented with a 7.62×51mm NATO version that would use standard NATO ammunition belts along with other features, but it never went into production. The Serbian Zastava M84 is a PK/PKS copy and the M86 a copy of the PKT. Arsenal in Bulgaria produced a copy of the PK designated MG-M1 and after joining NATO offered the MB-M2 in 7.62×51mm NATO. Romania's Cugir Mitralieră produces a copy of the PKM. Ukraine's Mayak KM-7.62 in various guises has seen continuous combat during the recent conflict with Russia (Smith 2007: 387).

Various of these Russian machine guns have been in continuous combat somewhere in the world since the end of World War II, with all indications that their distinctive sounds on full-automatic fire will echo for decades to come. Unlike tanks, aircraft, and artillery, machine guns require only the weapon, ammunition, and a couple of fighters to send death down range.

Iraqi troops practice-firing the Pusca Mitralieră md. 1964, Romania's RPK derivative, from right and left shoulders at Habbaniyah, 2005. As the selector switch is on the right side, the soldier in the foreground will have to move his hand to operate the selector. Note also he has his hand on the magazine as if it is a foregrip. Applying pressure to the magazine can cause malfunctions. (USMC, courtesy the DTC/Wikimedia/Public Domain)

CONCLUSION

Before writing this section the author emailed a half-dozen friends who had either been military armorers or special operators who had to be familiar with non-US small arms and asked them: what word or phrase would you use to describe Russian machine guns? Their answers were quite similar. Some said "sturdy" or "durable," while others offered some variant of "soldier proof," "conscript proof," or "insurgent proof." Certainly, many members of the US and British armed forces, as well as other NATO members, might add the world "ubiquitous" based on the battlefields upon which they have faced fire from Russian machine guns.

Although "innovative" was not a word offered by those consulted, it does apply to the development of the RPD as an early squad automatic weapon, especially as it was chambered for the intermediate 7.62×39mm cartridge. Despite the wide distribution and use of the RPD in conflicts during the last three decades, however, it has faults. Its non-removable barrel leads to its overheating if fired continuously in combat. The location of the drum magazine also proves inconvenient when firing and allows debris to enter the drum, though this issue was later addressed. Still, its ability to fire the same cartridge as the AK-47 made the RPD the perfect weapon for Soviet surrogates for decades, and it remains in use in trouble spots around the world.

To replace the RPD, the Soviet Union continued to use the 7.62×39mm cartridge in the RPK; in effect, an automatic rifle much as the United States had used for decades in the form of the Browning Automatic Rifle (BAR). Its use of the Kalashnikov system, controls, and magazines offered advantages to Soviet troops, but there were also disadvantages in terms of caliber, ability to sustain fire, and range. Though ostensibly the RPK's use of box magazines instead of a belt feed might seem a disadvantage for sustained fire, RPD ammunition belts were problematical and resulted in stoppages. Arguably, too, the time required to change box magazines offered some cooling time between bursts of fire. Though, theoretically,

This "Technical" in Mogadishu, Somalia, *c*.1992–93, has a KPV and other Soviet-era machine guns among its armament. (CT Snow/Wikimedia/CC BY-SA 2.0)

the RPK's 75-round drum avoided some of the disadvantages of the box magazines, in reality it proved unreliable, heavy, and prone to rattle; hence, the drum was rarely used. Nevertheless, the RPK in the form of the RPK-74 continues as the primary Russian squad automatic weapon during the Russia–Ukraine conflict.

The PK/PKM has proven an effective GPMG and remains in service today. It might be argued that it is archaic in its retention of a non-disintegrating ammunition belt and the 7.62×54mmR cartridge, but it continues to see combat in Ukraine and elsewhere. With the help of modern optics, both day and night, the PKMN/PKMSN can optimize the range of the 7.62×54mmR cartridge. The combination of the use of stampings and its proven reliability has made the PKM a cost-effective weapon. The Pecheneg addresses criticisms of the PKM's accuracy due to its forced-air-cooled barrel, which incorporates radial ribs, and a handle that helps mitigate impaired target acquisition due to the release of hot gases from the barrel.

Russian reliance on artillery in World War II – the "Red God of War" – may have also influenced Russian use of HMGs. Prior to the development of portable antiaircraft missiles (i.e. MANPADS), HMGs provided antiaircraft defense for vehicles and bodies of infantry in the Soviet armed forces. Combat in Afghanistan also dictated the use of the longer-ranged and harder-hitting HMGs to defend roads or engage Mujahideen fighters ensconced on the heights.

The 12.7×108mm DShK entered service prior to World War II, though only 9,000 were produced during that conflict. Estimates are that 1 million examples have been produced up to the time of writing and the weapon continues to see use today, especially with Ukrainian forces, which have found various ways to repurpose it as a drone killer or in unmanned, remotely fired ambush sites. In the hands of insurgents such as the PAVN/VC or the Mujahideen, the *Dushka* proved a portable and cost-effective "helicopter killer."

While the United States has continued to use the .50-caliber M2 Browning HMG for more than 90 years, the weapon has undergone several upgrades, with the M2HB (Heavy Barrel) being the current standard HMG; in contrast, Russia has continued the development of new HMGs. In the case of the KPV/KPVT, Russia developed a "heavy, heavy" machine gun. The 14.5×114mm KPV remains in use primarily in the

A 2014 view of a Pecheneg. (Vitaly V. Kuzmin/Wikimedia/ CC BY-SA 3.0)

A US Marine undergoing weapons familiarization training with a PK variant during 2019. (USMC/Public Domain)

KPVT version mounted on the BTR-60B and BTR-79 armored personnel carriers and BRDM armored reconnaissance vehicles.

Other 12.7×108mm HMGs have replaced the DShKM for most frontline missions involving Russian troops. The NSV and NSVT are lighter than the DShKM and may be handled by a two-man infantry crew along with the tripod. The NSV is also equipped with optical sights, allowing more effective use in either the antiaircraft/antidrone role or for infantry support. Even more effective for infantry use is the Kord, which is designed to reduce recoil substantially.

The durability of Russian machine guns in use around the world must also be acknowledged. At the time of writing, in conflicts still raging in places such as Somalia and the Amhara region of Ethiopia, the RPD is still in combat more than 80 years after it was introduced during World War II. The DShK, which was introduced even earlier in 1938, is seeing action in Gaza and Ukraine. Variants of the RPK remain important weapons in combat in Gaza and Ukraine and remain in production and use by countries formerly and/or currently within the Russian sphere of influence. Major users of the PKM include Bangladesh, China, India, Indonesia, and North Korea, among others. China, India, and North Korea have produced or are producing versions of the PK/PKM. While most users of the PKM continue to use the 7.62×54mmR cartridge, now in its third century of service, some examples produced in countries such as China chamber the NATO-standard 7.62×51mm round.

As durable as Russian machine-gun designs have been, development has continued on new designs such as the 5.45×39mm RPL-20 from Kalashnikov Concern. Note, however, that the RPL-20 would be a squad automatic weapon, and an improvement on the RPK-74, rather than a new GPMG.

As these final words are written, Russian machine guns are "bursting" away in Ukraine, Gaza, Sudan, and elsewhere. Given the millions of Russian machine guns in front-line service or reserve, that situation will likely continue for decades to come.

BIBLIOGRAPHY

Anonymous (2019). "Forgotten Soviet cartridge 6×49mm vs cartridge 6,8 mm NSGW," *Top War*, November 19, 2019. https://en.topwar.ru/164855-zabytyj-sovetskij-patron-6h49-mm-protiv-patrona-68-mm-ngsw.html

Anonymous (2021). "Chinese air defense systems in the Korean War," *Top War*, September 30, 2021. https://en.topwar.ru/187478-kitajskie-sredstva-pvo-v-korejskoj-vojne.html

Anonymous (2022a). "Ukrainian Gunmen Mounted a 12.7mm 'Utyos' Machine Gun on a Pickup to 'Bring Nightmare' to Russians," *Defense Express*, July 20, 2022. https://en.defence-ua.com/weapon_and_tech/ukrainian_gunmen_mounted_a_127mm_utyos_machine_gun_on_a_pickup_to_bring_nightmare_to_russians-3626.html

Anonymous (2022b). "Russia is Converting Salvaged Russian PKTs," *The Armourer's Bench*, March 27, 2022. https://armourersbench.com/2022/03/27/ukraine-is-converting-salvaged-russian-pkts/

Anonymous (2023). "Machine gun 'KORD' is being upgraded," *Top War*, June 9, 2023. https://en.topwar.ru/218872-pulemet-kord-prohodit-modernizaciju.html

Besedovskyy, Vlad (2023a). "PK or PKM? Choice of a Soviet machinegunner in Afghanistan," February 18, 2023. https://www.safar-publishing.com/post/pk-or-pkm-choice-of-a-soviet-machinegunner-in-afghanistan

Besedovskyy, Vlad (2023b). "RPK and RPK-74 Soviet LMGs in Soviet-Afghan War," April 8, 2023. https://www.safar-publishing.com/post/rpk-and-rpk-74-soviet-lmgs-in-soviet-afghan-war

Bouzid, A. (1996). "Summary of Armament During the 1954 Revolution." https://digitalarchive.wilsoncenter.org/document/bouzid-summary-armament-during-1954-revolution

Cleary, C. & J. Cusack (1999). "Machine-gun find believed to be part of IRA arsenal," *The Irish Times*, January 15, 1999. https://www.irishtimes.com/news/machine-gun-find-believed-to-be-part-of-ira-arsenal-1.146078

Department of the Army (1984). *The Soviet Army: Operations and Tactics*. FM 100-2-1. Washington, DC: Department of the Army.

Golembesky, Michael (2016). *Dagger 22: US Marine Corps Special Operations in Bala Murghab, Afghanistan*. New York, NY: St. Martin's Press.

Gosselin-Malo, Elisabeth (2024). "Ukrainian forces rig machine gun networks to down Russian drones," *Defense News*, April 5, 2024. https://www.defensenews.com/global/europe/2024/04/05/ukrainian-forces-rig-machine-gun-networks-too-down-russian-drones/

Grau, Lester W. & Charles K. Bartles (2016). *The Russian Way of War: Force Structure, Tactics, and Modernization of the Russian Ground Forces*. Fort Leavenworth, KS: Foreign Military Studies Office. https://www.armyupress.army.mil/portals/7/hot%20spots/documents/russia/2017-07-the-russian-way-of-war-grau-bartles.pdf

Grau, Lester W. & Charles K. Bartles (2022). "Getting to Know the Russian Battalion Tactical Group," RUSI, April 14, 2022. https://www.rusi.org/explore-our-research/publications/commentary/getting-know-russian-battalion-tactical-group

Guttman, Jon (2019). "TBT: The inside story of the Soviet Red Army's RPD machine gun," *Military Times*, December 19, 2019. https://www.militarytimes.com/off-duty/gearscout/irons/2019/12/19/tbt-the-inside-story-of-the-soviet-red-armys-rpd-machine-gun/

Heebum Hong & Dan Shea (2023). "North Korean Small Arms," *Small Arms Defense Journal*, August 11, 2023. https://sadefensejournal.com/north-korean-small-arms/

Isby, David C. (1988). *Weapons and Tactics of the Soviet Army*. London: Jane's.

Isby, David C. (1989). *War in a Distant Country*. London: Arms & Armour.

Jones, Richard D., ed. (2007). *Jane's Infantry Weapons, 2007–2008*. Alexandria, VA: Jane's.

Litovkin, Nikolai (2020). "Russia creates a new machine gun for special forces," *Russia Beyond*, September 3, 2020. https://www.rbth.com/science-and-tech/332661-kalashnikov-creates-new-machine-gun

Meyerle, Jerry & Carter Malkasian (2009). "Insurgent Tactics in Southern Afghanistan 2002–2008." Marine Corps Intelligence Activity. https://ia601300.us.archive.org/34/items/AfghanInsurgentTactics/AfghanInsurgentTactics.pdf

Nawroz, Gen. Mohammad Yahya & Lester W. Grau (1995). "The Soviet War in Afghanistan: History and Harbinger of Future War?" *Military Review*, September/October 1995. https://archive.org/details/1995_10_01_The_Soviet_War_in_Afghanistan_History_and_Harbinger_of_Future_War_Nawroz_and_Grau

Newton, Simon (2022). "Dushka: The Ukrainian military's modified Soviet-built machine gun," *Forces News*, September 6, 2022. https://www.forcesnews.com/technology/weapons-and-kit/dushka-ukrainian-militarys-modified-soviet-built-machine-gun

Oliker, Olga (2001). "Russia's Chechen Wars 1994–2000: Lessons from Urban Combat." Rand Corporation. https://www.rand.org/pubs/monograph_reports/MR1289.html

Ortiz, Miguel (2022). "Ukraine converted .50 caliber machine guns into shoulder-fired infantry weapons," *We Are the Mighty*, August 22, 2022. https://www.wearethemighty.com/articles/ukraine-converted-50-caliber-machine-guns-into-shoulder-fired-infantry-weapons/

Pelletiere, Stephen C. & Douglas V. Johnson II (1991). "Lessons Learned: The Iran–Iraq War." US Army War College. https://apps.dtic.mil/sti/pdfs/ADA232451.pdf

Plaster, John L. (2020). "Behind Enemy Lines: Guns of Vietnam's SOG Warriors," *American Rifleman*, April 7, 2020. https://www.americanrifleman.org/content/behind-enemy-lines-guns-of-vietnam-s-sog-warriors/

Popenker, Maxim & Anthony G. Williams (2008). *Machine Gun: The Development of the Machine Gun from the Nineteenth Century to the Present Day*. Ramsbury: Crowood.

Rempfer, Kyle (2018). "SOCOM solicitation for 'reverse engineered' foreign weapons sparks Russian anger, warnings," *Air Force Times*, October 16, 2018. https://www.airforcetimes.com/news/your-air-force/2018/10/16/socom-solicitation-for-reverse-engineered-foreign-weapons-sparks-russian-anger-warnings/

Roblin, Sebastien (2021). "Why Russia's DShK Machine Gun Is Fighting Around the World," *The National Interest*, April 25, 2021. https://nationalinterest.org/blog/reboot/why-russias-dshk-machine-gun-fighting-around-world-183536

Roblin, Sebastien (2023). "Captured Manual Reveals Russia's New 'Assault Detachment' Doctrine," *Forbes*, February 28, 2023. https://www.forbes.com/sites/sebastienroblin/2023/02/28/captured-manual-reveals-russias-new-assault-detachment-doctrine/?sh=7718eb54bb39

Russian General Staff, trans. Michael A. Gress & ed. Lester W. Grau (2002). *The Soviet–Afghan War: How a Superpower Fought and Lost*. Lawrence, KS: University Press of Kansas.

Stanton, Doug (2009). *Horse Soldiers: The Extraordinary Story of a Band of US Soldiers Who Rode to Victory in Afghanistan*. New York, NY: Scribner.

Thomas, Timothy L. (2007). "Russian Tactical Lessons Learned Fighting Chechen Separatists," *Journal of Slavic Military Studies* 18.4: 731–66.

Thompson, Henry L. (2023). *SOG Codename Dynamite: A MACV-SOG 1-0's Personal Journal*. Watkinsville, GA: Wormhole Publishing.

US Army (1967). *US Army Special Forces Foreign Weapons Handbook*. https://apps.dtic.mil/sti/pdfs/AD0867982.pd

US Army (2004). Iraq: Small Arms Handbook. NGIC-1142-7005-05. National Ground Intelligence Center. https://weaponsdocs.wordpress.com/wp-content/uploads/2021/03/iraq_small_arms_handbook_1.pdf

Yousaf, Mohammad & Mark Adkin (2001). *Afghanistan: The Bear Trap*. PA: Casemate.

INDEX

Figures in **bold** refer to illustrations.

AEK-999 *Barsuk* GPMG 27
Afghan wars, use in 5, 26, 40–41, 44–47, 53, 54–56, **55**, **56**, 67, 71: Mujahideen fighters 4, 40, 41, **42–43**, 44, 46, 47, 49, 55, 76
AFVs, mounting on 4, 9, 15–16, **16**, 29, 62, 66, 72
Al-Quds LMG 48, 57, 73
Albania, copies/production 72, 73
Algerian War 36
Al-Qaeda 54
antiaircraft HMGs 8, 11, 12, 15, 16, 17, 33–34, 40, 44, 46, 49, 53, **53**, **56**, 77
antidrone HMGs 63–64, 71, 76, 77
antihelicopter machine guns 12, 41, 54, 55, 58, 76
antivehicle machine guns 33–34
APCs, mounting on 17, 23, 34, **35**, 46–47, 48, 62, 77
Ash-78 Tip-2 LMG 73

Bangladeshi forces, use by 77
"BB-Kalsh" LMG 48
British forces, use against 34, 56, 75
Bulgaria, copies/production 73, 74

Chechen Wars, use in 5, **5**, 26, 49, **49**, 52–53, **52**, 53, 60, **61**, 62, 66
China, copies/production 15, 37, 40, 46, 72, 74, 77
Chinese forces, use by 33–34, 60, 62, 72
CS/LM4 GPMG 74
Czechoslovakia, copies/production 72

DA LMG 7
DK HMG 11
DP LMGs 4, 6, 7, 11–12, 13, 14, 37
DPM LMG 7, 13, 18
drones, mounting on 64
DS-39 MMG 4, 8
DShK/DShKM HMGs 8, 11, 12, 13, 28, 29, 30, 39: copies/production 33, 60, 72; features/production 12, **39**, 48, **64**; use/users 12, **13**, 17, 29, 33–34, 40, 41, **42–43**, 44, 45, 46, 48, **48**, 53, 54, 56, 57, 58, 62, 63, **64**, 66, 68, 71, 76, 77
DShK-38/-38-46 HMGs 4, 12, 32
DT LMG 7, 34

East Germany production/use 10, **72**, 74
Egypt, production/use 6, 9, 34, 72
Ethiopia, use in 67, 77

Finnish forces, use by 23, **28**, 69
First Indochina War, use in 33
FN MAG GPMG 45, 68, 70
FN Minimi LMG 22, 31, 37, 45, 51, 68

helicopters, mounting on 4, 46, **52**, 54, 66
Hungarian forces, use by 73
Hungarian Revolution, use in 34, **35**

IFVs, mounting on 40, 47, 60, **61**, 66
Indonesian forces, use by 77
Iran, copies/production 70, 72
Iran–Iraq War, use in 10, 48, 67
Iranian forces, use by 10, 48
Iraq, copies/production 48, 57, 73
Iraqi forces, use by 4, 26, 48, 57–58, **57**, **58**, **59**, 71, **74**
Iraqi insurgents, use by 57–58
ISIS insurgents, use by 60, **60**, **61**, 62

Kord HMG 29, 30, **30**, 53, 60, **61**, 62, 66, 71, 77
Korean War, use in 33–34, 48
KPV HMG 15–17, 28, 41, 44, 54, 56, 58, **75**, 76–77

KPVT HMG 16, **16**, 17, 45, 53, 76, 77
Kurdish militiamen, use by **59**, **62**
KVT HMG 47

LMG-F LMG 73
LMGK LMG **72**, 74

M2/M2HB HMG 12, 17, 34, 76
M60 GPMG 38, 68
M72 LMG 74
M72B1 LMG 73
M84 GPMG 74
M86 74
M240 GPMG 31, 45, 57, 70–71
M249 SAW 22, 31, 45, 51, 57, 68
Mayak KM-7.62 GPMG 74
MB-M2/MG-M1 GPMGs 74
MG-1M GPMG 57
MG 13 LMG 9
MG 30 Solothurn LMG 9
MG 34 GPMG 9–10, 23
MG 42 GPMG 5, 9, 10, 23
MG3 GPMG **10**, 68
MGD 12.7 HMG 48, 72
motorcycles, mounting on 10, 62
MT-LB HMG 62
MTPU HMG 16

North Korea, production/use 33–34, 57, 60, **72**, 77
North Vietnam forces, use by 37
Northern Ireland, use in 6, 54
NSV *Utyos* HMG 28–29, **29**, 30, 47, 64: use/users 29, 45, 47, 62, **69**, 71, 77
NSV N3/-12.7/-12.7 N4 HMGs **28**, 29
NSVT HMG 29, 77

Pakistan, copies/production 72
patrol boats/light craft, mounting on 16
Pecheneg/Pecheneg-SP GPMGs 26, 27, **27**, 76, 76: use/users 60, **61**, 62
Peruvian forces, use by 54
PK GPMG 10, 23, 26, 27, 52, 63, 65: copies 74; features 26; use/users 5, **26**, 43, 44, 48, 52, 53, 55, 56, 57, 58, **58**, 59, 60, 62, 65, 70, 74, 76, 77
PKB/PKC machine gun 23, **52**, 58
PKM GPMG 18, 26, 27, 31, 60, 63, 70–71, 76: copies 74; features 23, **24–25**, 45; use/users 23, 32, 40, 43, 44–45, 45, 46, 47, 48, 49, 52, 53, 54, 56, 57, 58, 59, 62, 63, 65, 65, 69, 70–71, 73, 74, 76, 77
PKMN GPMG 76
PKMS GPMG 26, 45, 70, 74
PKMSN GPMG 76
PKMT GPMG 30
PKN GPMG 27
PKS GPMG 23, 26, 48, 58, 74
PKSN GPMG 27
PKT machine gun 23, 57, 74: use/users 40, 47, 48, 57, **57**, 66
PKZ GPMG 27
PM M1910 and M1910/30 MMGs 4, 6, 7, 7, 8, 13, 63
PN1 machine gun 23
Poland, copies by 74
Pusca Mitralierǎ md. 1964/1993 LMGs 74. **74**

RBK LMG 57; Red Army, use by 6, 7, 32
remote weapon stations 17, 76: 6C21 30
Romania, copies/production 72, 73–74, **74**
RP-46 LMG 12, 13
RPD LMG 11, 14–15, **14**, 18, 19, 23, 71, 75: copies/production 33, 34, 36, 40, 72; features 15, **32**, 33, **36**; use/users 5, 15, 32, 34, 35, 36–37, 36, 38, **38**, 39, 40, 41, 43, 46, 51, 67, 68, 69, 70, 72–73, 75

RPDM LMG 14
RPK LMG 10, 15, 18–19, 26, 50–51, 75–76: copies/production 48, 57, 72, 73–74, **73**, **74**; features **18**, **20–21**; use/users 4, 39, 40, 43, 44, 45, 47, 52, 53, 55, 56, 57, 58, 67, **67**, 68–69, 75; RPK-16 LMG 22
RPK-74 LMG 18, **19**, 26, 31, 50–51, 77: use/users 40, **42**, 44, 45, 47, **50**, 51, 52, 67, 68–69, 76
RPK-74M/-74N2 LMGs 18, **19**
RPKN LMG 18, **22**
RPKS/RPKS-74/RPKSN LMGs 18, 44, 46
RPL-20 LMG 31, **31**, 77
Russia–Ukraine War, use in 5, 7, 7, 10, 12, **13**, **30**, 63–64, **63**, **64**, 65–66, **66**, 67, 71, 72, 74, 76, 77
Russian/Soviet Army, use by 4–5, 12, 32, 35, 37, 40–41, **42–43**, 44–47, 49, 63, 71, 76, 77
 airborne/airmobile 26, 27, 31, 40, 44, 47
 assault companies/platoons 64, 66
 assault groups 52
 fire-support platoons 66
 infantry squads 51
 military police 60, **61**
 motor-rifle troops 34, 40, 45, 46, 47
 MVD/OMON troops 27, 30, **52**, **67**
 parachute companies 46
 spetsnaz 18, 44, 52, 60

SG-43 MMG 4, 8, 9, **9**, 37, 43
SGM MMG 8, 37
SGMB MMG 34, **35**
SGMT MMG 8, 23
Somalia, use in 53, 75, 77
Sudan, use in 77
Suez Crisis, use in 34
Syrian Civil War, use in 17, 32, 60, **60**, **61**, 62, **62**, 67, 68, 77

tanks, mounting on 7, 8, **12**, 15–16, 23, 29, 30, 34, 40, 41, 45, 46, 47, 48, 54–56, 57, 57, 66, 74
"Technicals"/trucks, mounting on 12, 17, 34, 46, 53, 58, 64, 75
Tigr-M HMG 62; TK Vz.53 HMG 72
TUL-1 LMG 40
Type 7.62 LMG 72
Type 50 MMG 37
Type 54 HMG 33, 39, 72
Type 56 LMG 33, 36, 40, 72
Type 56-1 LMG 72
Type 57 MMG 37
Type 62 72
Type 73 LMG 57
Type 80/82 GPMGs 57, 74

Ukrainian forces, use by 5, 7, 7, 12, **13**, 30, 63–64, **63**, **64**, 65–66, **66**, 71, 72, 74, 76, 77
US forces, use by 4, 15, 48, 54, 55, 56, 58, 68, 75
 coaching of Iraqi troops 57, 58
 familiarization with **13**, 38, 39, 54, 57, 58, 64, 66, 67, **69**, 70–71, 77
 Vietnam War 36, **38**, **39**, 40: MACV-SOG operators 38, 73; SOG teams 38–39

Vietnam War, use in 28, 67: ARVN 40; PAVN/VC 12, 15, 33, 36, 37, 38–40, 76; US forces 15, 36, 38–39, **38**, **39**, 40, 54, 55, 56, 58, 73

W85 HMG 60, 62
Wagner Group 64, 70

Yugoslavia, copies/production 60, **73**

ZPU HMG 16
ZPU-1 HMG **56**
ZSU-23-4 *Shilka* SPAAG 46, 49, 53